Jeanne Marie Bouvier de La Motte Guyon

The Worship of God in Spirit and in Truth

Jeanne Marie Bouvier de La Motte Guyon

The Worship of God in Spirit and in Truth

ISBN/EAN: 9783742824011

Manufactured in Europe, USA, Canada, Australia, Japa

Cover: Foto ©Lupo / pixelio.de

Manufactured and distributed by brebook publishing software (www.brebook.com)

Jeanne Marie Bouvier de La Motte Guyon

The Worship of God in Spirit and in Truth

THE
Worship of GOD,
IN
Spirit and in Truth:
OR, A
Short and easy Method of Prayer,

Suited to *every* Capacity;

With Two Letters upon the same Subject.

By Madam GUION.

To which is added,
TWO LETTERS,
Concerning a Life truly Christian;

And a DISCOURSE upon the *universal* Love and Goodness of GOD to Mankind, in and through Jesus Christ.

Extracted from Two late Authors.

BRISTOL:
Printed by W. PINE, for T. MILLS, Bookseller, in Wine-Street, 1775.

THE
Author's PREFACE.

A Great many persons have fancied Prayer and Devotion *to be things so very frightful and extraordinary, that they thought it was but in vain to labour to acquire them, despairing ever to be able to compass them. But as the* difficulty *which one apprehends to be in any thing maketh him despair of being able to succeed in it, and at the same time stifleth his desire of undertaking it; so on the other hand, when one proposes to himself a thing as advantageous, and which is easy to be obtained, he sets about it with pleasure, and carries it on with resolution: this is what hath obliged us to discover both the advantage and facility of this method. O! were we but perswaded of the* infinite goodness of God *toward his poor creatures, and of the desire that he hath to communicate himself to them, we should not apprehend such difficulties, neither should we so easily despair to obtain a good which he desireth so earnestly to give us.*

After that he hath given us his only Son, and delivered him to the death for us. Rom. viii. 32. *How can he refuse us any thing else? No surely: We want but a little* courage and perseverance. *We have so much of both for our little temporal interests, and yet almost none at all left for the* one thing necessary, Luke x. 42.

I am willing that such as have difficulty to believe, that 'tis easy to find God in this manner, do not believe what is here told them: but let them make the experiment of it, and then let them judge for themselves, and they shall see that there is but very little told them, in comparison of what the thing really is. Read therefore, dearest reader, this small Treatise with a simple and sincere heart, with childlike littleness and humility of spirit, and you'll find very much good by it. Receive it with the same spirit that we give it you, which is no other but to carry you wholly to God without reserve. Our design is

to

to encourage the simple and the little ones to go to their father who loveth their humble confidence, and whom distrust very much displeaseth. Seek not for any thing in it but the love of God, and retain always a sincere desire of your salvation, and ye shall certainly find it.

We don't at all pretend to raise our opinion above that of others, but we sincerely declare the experience we have had, both in ourselves and others, of the advantage that there is to be found in the use of this plain and simple manner of going to God. If we pass by several things which are esteemed, and speak only of the short and easy method of prayer, it is because the treatise being intended only for this, it can't so well treat of any thing else.

It is certain that whosoever reads it in the same spirit in which it was written, will find nothing that's shocking or uneasy; they will be farther confirmed in the truth which it contains, would they but make a competent trial of it.

It belongeth to thee, O blessed JESUS! who lovest simplicity, and who takest

takest thy delights in being with the children of men, Prov. vii. 31, *that is, with those amongst men, who are truly willing to become children:* it belongeth to thee, I say, to give the due value and esteem to this little work, by imprinting it on the heart, and inclining those who shall read it, to seek thee in their heart where thou desirest to receive the marks of their love, and to give them the testimonies of thine. They deprive themselves of these good things by their own fault. It is thy work, O thou God of love! O thou silent WORD! 'tis thy work to make thyself to be beloved, tasted, and heard. Thou canst do it, and I am confident thou wilt do it to the soul that gives itself up to thee.

Glory be to thy name for ever.

CONTENTS.

	Page
M. GUION's *preface* - -	3
Section I.	
That all have ability to pray -	7
Section II.	
Of the right manner of prayer -	13
Section III.	
For those who cannot read - -	20
Section IV.	
Of the second degree of prayer -	26
Section V.	
Of spiritual drinesses - -	28
Section VI.	
Of resignation - - -	31

Section

CONTENTS.

　　　　　　　　　　　　　　Page

Section VII.
Of sufferings - - - - 35

Section VIII.
Of the mysteries of our redemption through Jesus Christ - - 38

Section IX.
Of virtue - - - 41

Section X:
Of mortification - - - 43

Section XI.
Of conversion - - - 47

Section XII.
Of the prayer of God's simple presence - - - 52

Section XIII.
Of rest before God - - 60

Section XIV.
Of the inward silence - - 62

Section XV.
Of self-examination: and of confession - - - 65

CONTENTS.

Page

Section XVI.
Of reading and of vocal prayers - 71

Section XVII.
Of petitions - 72

Section XVIII.
Of defects or infirmities - 74

Section XIX.
Of distractions and temptations - 76

Section XX.
Of true prayer and adoration - 78

Section XXI.
That one acts more vigorously and more nobly by this manner of prayer than by any other - 83

Section XXII.
Of internal acts - 101

Section XXIII.
An address to pastors and preachers 114

Section XXIV.
What is the safest method to arrive at the divine union - 124

Letter

CONTENTS.

Page

Letter I.
Madam Guion to Mr. B. of London 142

Letter II.
Madam Guion to Mrs. T. of London 155

Extracted from two late Authors.

1   Letter I.
Concerning a life truly Christian 161

2   Letter II.
Describing some of the temptations which attends a life truly Christian 177

3. A Discourse *upon the univerfal love and goodness of God to mankind in and through Jesus Christ* - - - - 187

ERRATA.

Page 131, read after *he addeth,* that *the perſon whoſe works ſhall be found fit to be burnt, ſhall be ſaved; yet ſo as by fire.*

N. B. The PUBLISHER is ſenſible that there are ſeveral other errors of the preſs, as well as in the punctuation, which he is perſuaded the Reader's good ſenſe will correct and candor pardon.

☞ Madam Guion's enemies made her *Short and Eaſy Method of Prayer*, a pretext for her PERSECUTION, IMPRISONMENT, and EXILE. Vide ſupplement to Lady Guion's Life, page 269, and her Letters, No. 158, 159, &c. publiſhed with the *Diſſertation* on PURE LOVE, written by the ARCHBISHOP of CAMBRAY.

A Short and Easy Method OF PRAYER.

Sect. I.

That all have ability to pray.

ALL men are capable of *prayer*; and therefore 'tis a dreadful unhappiness that generally all persons almost do imagine that they are not called to prayer. But we are all called to prayer, like as we are all called to salvation.

Prayer

Prayer is no other thing but the *application of the heart to God,* and the *inward exercife of love.* St. Paul enjoins us to *pray without ceafing* 1 Theff. v. 17. And our Lord faith *I fay unto you all, watch and pray.* Mark xiii. 33, 37. All then may pray, and all ought to pray. But I confefs, all cannot meditate, and that but very few are fitted for it. So it is not this prayer of meditation which God requires, nor which we defire of you, my deareft brethren, whofoever you be that would be faved. Come ye therefore every one to pray; ye ought to live by prayer, as ye ought to live by love. *I counfel you to buy of me gold tried in the fire, that you may be rich.* Rev. iii. 18. It is moft eafy for you to obtain it, yea, more than you can imagine. *Come all ye that are athirft unto thefe living waters; and don't amufe yourfelves to hew out broken*

broken cisterns that can hold no water. Jo. vii. 37. Jer. ii. 13. Come all ye hungry hearts, which find not any thing that can content you, and you shall be fully satisfied. Come ye poor afflicted ones, ye who are oppressed with trouble and sorrows, and ye shall be comforted. Come ye that are sick to your Physician, and fear not to approach him because you are weighed down with maladies: lay open to him all your diseases, and ye shall be relieved. Come ye children to your Father, and he will receive you with the arms of love Come ye poor wandring and stragling sheep, draw nigh to your Shepherd. Come ye sinners near to your Saviour. Come ye dull and ignorant ones, ye are all fit for prayer, even ye who think yourselves incapable thereof, are most of all fitted for it. Come all of you
without

without exception, Jesus Christ calleth you all. Yet let not those who are without an heart come, for they only are dispens'd from coming; for there must be an heart to love. But who is without an heart? O come then and give this heart unto God; and learn the manner of doing it. All who are willing to pray can easily do it with the assistance of the ordinary graces, and of the gifts of the Holy Spirit, which are common to all Christians.

Prayer is the key to supreme happiness. It is the effectual means of delivering us from all vices, and of acquiring all virtues: for the great means of becoming perfect, is to walk in the presence of God. This he said himself, *Walk in my presence, and be perfect.* Gen. xvii. 1. 'Tis prayer alone that can give you this presence, and that can give it you continually.

Therefore

Therefore you must learn a kind of prayer which can be made at all times, which doth not divert from outward business, and which princes, kings, prelates, priests, magistrates, soldiers, children and labourers, women and sick persons, may all perform. This is not the prayer of the head, but the prayer of the heart. It is not a prayer of thought only, because the spirit of man is so bounded, that while he thinks on one thing, he can't think on another; but it is the prayer of the heart, which is not at all interrupted by all the occupations of the mind: nothing but irregular affections can interrupt the prayer of the heart; and 'tis almost impossible for the soul which has once tasted God, and the sweetness of his love, to relish any thing else but him.

There's nothing more easy, than

to have God, and to taste (or delight in) him. He is more in us than we ourselves. He desires more to give himself to us, than we do to possess him. All consists in the right manner of seeking him, which yet is so easy and so natural, that the very air which we breathe is not more so. And even you who think yourselves so dull, as that you are not good for any thing; you (I say) may live by prayer, and upon God himself, as easily and as continually as ye live by the air which you breathe. Shall ye not then be highly criminal if ye don't do it? But doubtless ye will do it when ye shall have learned the way, which is indeed the the easiest that can be.

Sect. II.

Sect II.

Of the right Manner of Prayer.

THERE are two ways of introducing fouls into prayer, which they may and ought to ufe for a certain time. The one is, *Meditation*; the other is, *Meditation upon Reading*.

Meditation upon Reading is nothing elfe, but to take fome weighty truths, which afford matter both for fpeculation and practice; but efpecially for the latter, and to proceed in this manner. *Firft*, You fhall take the truth, fuch as you are pleafed to chufe, and read two or three lines of it in order, that you may tafte and digeft them, endeavouring to draw out the juice or substance of them, and to *keep fix'd to the place* which you read, *so long as you find any relish* in it, not passing further till that place become insipid unto you.

Then you must take as much more, and do just the same, not reading above half a page at a time: for it is not so much the quantity of reading that is profitable, as the manner of reading. Hence those who run apace cannot improve by what they read, any more than the bees can draw out the juice of the flowers by flying over them, without resting upon them. To read much, serves more for school-learning than for spiritual knowledge: but to profit really by spiritual books, they must be read in the manner above expressed; and I'm sure, that if any did so, they would by reading gradually accustom themselves

to

to prayer, and become very much dispos'd for it.

The other (help to prayer) is, *Meditation*, which is performed in a season set apart for it, and not in the time of reading. I think it might be good to enter upon it in this manner. After having placed yourself in the presence of God. by an act of faith, you must read something that's substantial, and stop gently upon it; not that you may reason, but only to fix your mind; remembering that the principal exercise ought to be the presence of God, and that the subject should serve more to stay your mind than to employ your reason. A firm belief of God being present in the ground of our hearts, must needs engage us to sink down into ourselves, gathering all the thoughts inward, and hindering them from being scattered abroad; which is a powerful means of ridding us from a multitude of distractions, and of removing us far from outward objects, that we may approach unto God, who cannot be found but in the inward ground of ourselves, and in our centre, which is the *Holy of Holies*, where he dwells. Yea, he promises that *if any man do his will, he will come unto him and make his abode in him.* Jo. xiv. 23. St. *Austin* accuses himself for the time which he had lost, in not having at first sought God after this manner.

When therefore any one is thus sunk and introverted into himself, and throughly penetrated with a living sense of the divine presence in his inward ground; when the thoughts are all gathered up and retir'd from the circumference to the

the centre; which indeed is somewhat painful in the beginning, but afterwards becomes moſt eaſy, as I ſhall ſhew you hereafter. When I ſay, the ſoul is thus recollected into itſelf, and when it is employed ſweetly and gently about the truth it hath read, not in reaſoning much upon it, but in favouring and taſting it, and in exciting the will by affection, rather than in applying the underſtanding by conſideration: the affection being thus ſtirred up, we muſt leave it to reſt ſweetly and in peace, that it may ſwallow down what it has taſted: for ſuppoſe one ſhould but chew an excellent bit, and indeed reliſh it, yet if he did not forbear a little this motion, ſo as to ſwallow it down, he could not be nouriſhed by it. So in like manner, when the affection is moved, if we would go on to move it ſtill, we

ſhould

should extinguish its fire, and thereby deprive the soul of its food; and therefore it must necessarily swallow down what it hath chew'd and tasted, by a little repose full of respect and confidence. This method is most necessary, and would advance a soul more in a little while, than any other is capable of doing in several years.

But as I have hinted, the principal exercise ought always to be the view of the divine presence: this also we ought to perform in the most faithful manner we can: to call in our thoughts whensoever they begin to wander. This is a short and effectual way to combat all distractions, because if any would oppose them directly, they but irritate and encrease them, whereas by sinking down in the view, and faith, of the divine presence, and simply recollecting ourselves,

selves, we combat them indirectly, and without thinking of them, though in a moft powerful manner.

I likewife admonifh all beginners not to run from one truth to another, or from one fubject to another; but to hold by one and the fame fo long as they find any relifh in it. This is the way quickly to enter and penetrate into the truths propofed, to tafte them, and to have them imprinted upon us.

I faid, 'tis difficult in the beginning for one to recollect himfelf, becaufe of the habit that the foul has gotten to be wholly without in things relating to the body; but when 'tis a little accuftom'd to recollection by the violence which it has done to itfelf, this becomes mighty eafy unto it; not only becaufe it acquires this habit, but alfo becaufe God, who feeks to commiunicate himfelf to his creature, fends it fuch abundant graces and fuch
an

an experimental taste of his presence, as render it most easy and delightful.

Sect III.

For those who cannot read.

THOSE who cannot read, are not hereby depriv'd of (the benefit of) prayer. JESUS CHRIST is the great book written without and within, which will teach them all things.

They ought to take this method: first, They must learn this fundamental truth, that *the kingdom of God is within them*; Luke xvii. 21. and that there it must be sought.

They who have the care of souls ought to teach their people to pray,
even

Method of Prayer. 21

even as they teach them the catechifm. They teach them the *end* for which they were created, but they don't fufficiently inftruct them how to come to the *enjoyment* of this end. I could wifh they would teach it them in this manner : namely, that they ought to begin by a profound act of adoration, and of felf-abafement before God, and therewith fhutting their bodily eyes, endeavour to open thofe of the foul ; then they are to gather it wholly inward, and to exercife themfelves directly with the prefence of God, by a lively faith that God is in us; not fuffering their thoughts and imaginations to wander abroad, but keeping them in captivity and fubjection as much as they are able.

Then let them fay thus the *Lord's Prayer* underftanding in fome meafure what they fay, and believing that God, who is within their foul,

is

is very willing to be their *Father*. Being in this difpofition, let them beg their neceffaries of him, and having pronounced this word FATHER, let them continue fome moments in filence with much reverence, waiting that this their heavenly Father may be pleafed to difcover unto them his will.

At other times, the Chriftian confidering himfelf as a child that's quite fpent, and all over filthy through his repeated falls, and who has no power either to ftand on his legs, or make himfelf clean, let him lay open his fhameful condition to his father in an humble manner, adding every now and then fome expreffions of love and regret, and again remaining in filence. Thereafter going on with the *Lord's Prayer*, let him pray this king of Glory to reign in him: giving up himfelf to him indeed, to the end that he may

Method of Prayer. 23

may do it, and furrendring to him the juft right which he hath over him.

If he perceive an Inclination to peace and filence, he ought not to proceed, but to abide in that ftate while it lafteth. After which he may go on to the next petition, *viz. Thy will be done in earth as it is done in heaven.* Mat. vi. 10. Whereupon thefe humble fuppliants are to defire that God may accomplifh all his will in them and by them: they muft give their heart and their liberty unto God, that he my difpofe thereof at his pleafure; and feeing that the peculiar work of the will fhould be to love, they muft defire to love, and afk of God his pure love. But this ought to be done in a calm and peaceful manner, and fo of the reft of the Lord's-Prayer; which the above-named perfons may very well teach them.

Again,

Again, They may place themselves as sheep before their shepherd, and ask of him their true substantial food. *O divine shepherd! Thou feedest thy sheep with thyself, and thou art their daily bread.*

They may also lay before him the necessities of their families: but all must be done in this direct and principal view of faith that God is within us.

Whatsoever men figure out or represent unto themselves as God, is not God; a lively faith of his presence is sufficient: for we must not form any image of God, tho' we may indeed of *Jesus Christ*; beholding him as a child, as crucified, or in any other state or mystery, provided that the soul do always seek him in its own centre. Again, We may consider him as our Physician, and present unto him our wounds, that

from

he may heal them: but still without any effort or violence, and with some little silence interposed from time to time, so that the silence may be mixed with action; thus by degrees increasing the silence, and lessening the discourse, until in the end by means of yielding gradually to the operation of God, he may get the ascendant in us; as we shall note hereafter.

When once the presence of God is given, and the soul begins by little and little to relish the silence and stillness, this experimental sense of the divine presence introduceth it into the second degree of prayer; which is attained both by such as can read, and such as cannot, by taking the method above described; tho' indeed God does favour some privileged souls with it even from the beginning.

Sect. IV.

Of the Second Degree of Prayer.

THIS we call the prayer of simplicity; for when the soul hath exercised itself for some time, as aforesaid, it feels by degrees that it can recollect itself more easily, and prayer becomes easy, sweet, and delightful; it knows now that this is the way to find *God*, for it feels the favour of his ointments. But then it must alter its method, and see to perform faithfully and couragiously what I am a going to say, without being troubled at what may be alledged concerning it.

First, So soon as the soul recollecteth and placeth itself in the presence of God with faith, let it con tinue thus a little in awful silence.

But if from the beginning, it feels some little sense of the divine presence, let it stop there without troubling itself about any thing, or proceeding further; and let it hold what is given it, so long as it lasteth. If this passeth away, then let it stir up its will by some tender affection; and if by the means of the first affection it finds itself placed again in its sweet peace, let it continue therein. We must blow the fire gently, and when it is once kindled, cease to blow it more; for if one should go on to blow still, he would but extinguish it.

I advise above all, that no one may ever conclude his prayer without continuing for some time towards the end in a respectful silence. 'Tis likewise of great importance for the soul to go to prayer with courage,

courage, and that it bring along with it a pure and difinterefted love: let it not go fo much to receive any thing from God, as to do his will. For a fervant who ferves his mafter only according as he rewards him, is indeed unworthy of any reward at all. Go therefore to prayer, not feeking any thing, but only to be as he pleafeth. This will preferve in you an evennefs of fpirit, and keep you from wondering either at God's repulfes, or your own drineffes.

Sect. V.

Of Spiritual Drynefs.

THOUGH God hath no other defire, but to communicate himfelf to the foul that loves and feeks

Method of Prayer.

seeks him; yet he often hideth himself, that he may rouze it from its lazinefs, and oblige it to feek after him with love and fidelity. But O! With what bounty doth he reward the faithfulnefs of his beloved foul? And how much are his withdrawings followed with divine confolations! Some are apt to think, that 'tis a greater fign of fidelity, and argues more of one's love, to feek him with the preffing efforts of the head, and the force of one's own activity; or that thefe will quickly make him return. No: believe me (dear fouls) this is not at all the conduct of this ftate of prayer; for 'tis neceffary, that with a loving patience, a contrite, lowly, and humble regard, a frequent, but peaceable affection, and a refpectful filence, ye wait for the return of your Beloved. You will let him fee, by this manner of acting, that 'tis him alone, and his good pleasure, that you love, and not the pleasure you may have in loving him. Therefore, *Be not impatient in the times of darkness, suffer the delays and suspensions of the consolations of God: be resigned under every state of mind, and thereby shall the divine life grow and be renewed,* Ecclus. ii. 1, 2, 3.

Be ye always patient in prayer, and though ye should not make any other all your life-time, but to wait in a humble, resign'd and contented spirit, for the return of your Beloved; Oh! you should pray to excellent purpose: in the mean time you might pour out some expressions of love. This way of proceeding doth mightily please God; and more powerfully prevails with him than any other!

SECT.

Sect. VI.

Of Resignation.

HERE resignation and the entire surrender of ourselves unto God must begin; namely, by being convinced, that whatsoever befals us from one moment to another, and whatsoever we want, is in the order and will of God. This conviction will render us content with every thing, and make us look upon all that happens to us as coming from God, and not from the creature. I earnestly beseech and conjure you my dearest brethren, whosoever you be that are willing indeed to give yourselves unto God, never to take back yourselves again, when ye have once given yourselves to him;

him; but believe, that a thing which is given away, is no more at your difpofal.

Refignation is that which is of the greateft confequence in the whole Chriftian path : nay, 'tis the key of the whole fpiritual life. Whofoever doth fully refign himfelf, fhall in a fhort time become perfectly united unto Chrift. We muft therefore keep firmly to refignation, without attending to reafoning fuggeftions. A great faith makes a great refignation: we ought to commit ourfelves unto God, *Hoping againft all hope*, Rom. iv. 18.

Refignation is a putting off all care of ourfelves, that we may leave all that concerns us entirely to the conduct of God. All Chriftians are exhorted thus to forfake and refign themfelves; for our Lord faid unto all in general, Matt.

Method of Prayer.

Matt. vi. 25. *Take ye no thought for the morrow: for your heavenly Father knoweth what ye stand in need of.* Prov. iii. 6. *Think on him in all thy ways, and he will direct thy paths.* Ch. xvi. 3. *Commit thy ways unto the Lord, aud he will establish thy thoughts.* Again, Pfalm xxxvii. 5. *Commit thy whole way unto the Lord: trust also in him, and he himself will do it.*

Our refignation then ought to be an entire forfaking and abandoning our all unto God, both with refpect to time and eternity forgetting ourfelves in a great meafure, and thinking on God only: by this means the heart remains always free, contented, and difengaged.

As to the practice of this virtue, it confifts in a continual forfaking and lofing all felf-will in the will of God; in renouncing all particular inclinations, how good foever they may seem to be, as soon as we feel them arise in us, that we may always stand in the indifference, willing only what God hath willed, and be indifferent as to all things that regard either the body or the soul, temporal or eternal goods; forgetting what is past, giving up the time present unto God, and leaving to his providence that which is to come; being contented with what happens every moment, seeing it brings along with it the eternal order of God concerning us, and which is a declaration of his will; not attributing any thing that befals us to the creature, but beholding all things in God, and considering them as coming infallibly from his hand, our own sin only excepted.

Suffer yourselves therefore to be governed by God, as it shall please him, both with respect

pect to your outward and inward
state.

Sect. VII.

Of Sufferings.

BE content to suffer whatsoever God shall see fit to lay upon you. If you love him purely, you will in this life seek him, as much on mount *Calvary*, as upon *Tabor*.

You must love him (I say) as much upon *Calvary* as *Tabor*, since that is the place where he discovers the most of his love.

Do not like to those Persons who give themselves unto him at one time, and take themselves back again at another. They give themselves up to be caressed, but they draw
back

back themselves again when they are crucified, or at least go to seek for their consolation in the creature.

No, no, (dear souls) you will never find true consolation, but in the love of the cross, and an entire resignation of your wills. *He that hath no relish of the cross, favoureth not the things that be of God!* Matt. xvi. 23. 'Tis impossible to love *God* without loving the cross; and indeed a heart which hath the relish of the cross, findeth even the most bitter things to be sweet, pleasant and delightful. *The hungry soul findeth bitter things sweet,* Prov. xxvii. 7. Because the more it hungers after God, the more doth it hunger after the cross. The cross bringeth the soul to God, and God giveth the cross to purify the soul.

The great sign of the internal ad-

advancement is, if one advanceth in the crofs. Refignation and the crofs go hand in hand together.

Whenfoever any thing occurs to which you feel a repugnancy refign yourfelves immediately to God with refpect to this very thing, and give up yourfelves as a facrifice unto him; then ye fhall fee that when the crofs cometh, it will not be fo very heavy, becaufe ye have willingly accepted it. Which notwithftanding will not keep you from feeling the weight of it; as fome imagine, that the feeling the crofs is not to fuffer: for to feel fuffering is one of the principal parts of fuffering itfelf. Jefus Chrift chofe to fuffer the utmoft fharpnefs of fufferings. We often bear the crofs in weaknefs, at other times with ftrength:

strength : all ought to be equal to us in the will of God.

Sect. VIII.

Of the Mysteries of our Redemption through *Jesus Christ.*

SOME may object unto me, that at this rate one cannot have any sense of the *mysteries* impressed upon him: but 'tis quite otherwise, for these are given in reality to the soul. *Jesus Christ* to whom we resign ourselves, and whom we follow as *the way,* whom we hear as *the truth,* and who animateth us as *the life,* Jo. xiv. 6. Uniting himself to the soul, makes it to bear all his several states. Now to *bear* the states or conditions of *Jesus Christ,* is a far greater thing than barely

Method of Prayer. 39

barely to *consider* the states of *Jesus Christ*. St. *Paul* did bear in his body the states of *Jesus Christ*. *I bear* (saith he) *in my body the marks of the Lord Jesus;* Gal. vi. 17. but he does not say that he reasoned upon them.

In this state of resignation, *Jesus Christ* often giveth us some views of his states after a very particular manner. Then it behoveth us to receive them, and to suffer our minds to be applied to any thing that pleaseth him; taking equally all the dispositions that he shall see fit to place us in, not chusing any one of ourselves but only this, of continuing always with him, of affectionately desiring him, and of giving up ourselves entirely to him; receiving with an evenness of mind all that he doth give us, whether light or darkness, fruitfulness or barrenness, strength or weakness,

weakness, sweetness, or bitterness, temptation, pains, troubles, or doubtings; nothing of all these should stop us. There are some persons whom God doth apply for the space of whole years to a feeling sense of some one or other of these mysteries. The simple view or thought of such a mystery, gathers them inwards; therefore they ought to be faithful to it: but when God removes it from them, then let them willingly be deprived of it. There be others who are troubled because they cannot think of any one mystery; but this is without reason, seeing that the affectionate attention of the mind to God, includeth all particular devotion: and whosoever is united to God alone by finding his rest in him, is indeed applied to all the mysteries in a more excellent manner. He that

that loves God, loveth every thing that proceedeth from him.

Sect. IX.
Of Virtue.

THIS is the short and certain way to acquire virtue; because God, being the principle of all virtue, to possess him is indeed to possess all virtue; and the nearer we approach unto this possession, the more we have of virtue in an eminent degree. Again, I say, that all virtue which is not given from within is but a mask of virtue and is like a garment which is put on or off at pleasure. But the virtue that is communicated from within is the only true essential and permanent virtue: *The beauty of the king's daughter cometh from within;* Pf. 44. 13, vulg. and of all people there are none who practise it more vigorously than these, tho' they do not think of the virtue in particular. For God, to whom they keep themselves united, makes them to perform it in all its kinds. O what hunger have these devout souls after sufferings! They think only on what may please their beloved, and so they begin to neglect themselves and contemn themselves: the more they love their God, the more do they hate themselves and disrelish the creatures. O if men could but learn this most easy method, which is fitted for every one, for the dull and ignorant as well as the learned, how easily would the whole church of God be reformed! There needs no more but to love. *Love* (faith St. *Austin*) *and do then what ye will.* For when we love indeed, we cannot will any thing that may displease

please our beloved. *God is love, and he that abideth in love dwelleth in God, and God in him.* 1 John iv. 16.

Sect. X.

Of Mortification.

I Say further, that 'tis next to impossible for one ever to arrive at the perfect mortification of his senses and passions by any other way than the love of God. The reason is very plain, for it is the soul that gives life and vigour to the senses; and likewise the senses which irritate and raise the passions. A dead man hath no more any sense or passion left in him because of the separation which is made betwixt the soul and the senses. All the labour which is done in the outward part carries still the soul more outwardly into the things to which it doth apply itself more strongly. It is in these things, that it exerts itself most: as for example: being applied directly to strictness and rigour in externals, it is wholly turned that way, and thereby invigorates the senses instead of mortifying them. For it is only from the application of the soul that the senses can draw any thing of force or vigour, and the more the soul is in them, the more doth it still enliven them. This life of sense doth move and provoke the passions, so far is it from extinguishing them. Austeries may well weaken the body, but can never blunt the edge or vigour of the senses, for the reason just now mention'd. One thing alone can do it, which is this, that the soul by the means of recollection

Method of Prayer. 45

tion be turn'd wholly inward or within itself, to the end it may be taken up with God, who is there present. If the soul turn all its vigour and force within itself it is separated from the senses by this very action alone, and so employing its whole force and strength within, it leaves, the senses without vigour; and the more it advances and approaches to God, the more it is separated and disjoyned from itself.

This is the reason why those persons in whom the attractions, of grace are strong, do find themselves wholly weakened in the outward man, so as many times to swoon or faint away. I don't by this mean, we ought not at all to mortify ourselves; no! for mortification must always accompany prayer, according to the measure of every ones strength, and circumstances. But I say, that none ought to make mortification their chief exercife, nor abfolutely to tie themfelves to fuch and fuch aufterities; but by fimply following the inward attraction and employing themfelves with the divine prefence, without thinking of mortification in particular, God does make them to undergo all forts of it: and he gives no refpite to the fouls that are faithful in furrendering themfelves unto him, until he has mortified in them all that remains there to be mortified.

Therefore we muft keep ourfelves only attentive to God. All perfons are not capable of outward aufterities, but all are capable of this. There are two of our fenfes, in the mortifying of which we cannot well exceed; namely, the feeing and the hearing; becaufe thefe take in the fpecies and ideas of things; bu

God doth it effectually, we need only to follow his Spirit.

The soul has a double advantage by observing this conduct; namely, that according as it withdraws from the outward, it still draws nearer unto God: and by approaching unto God, besides the secret power and virtue it receives which supports and preserves it, it necessarily departs as far from sin, as it approaches nearer to God; till at last it is brought to an habitual conversion.

Sect XI.

Of Conversion.

*T*URN *ye and be converted unto God in the bottom of your hearts, according as you have deeply revolted from him,* Isa. xxxi. 6. vulg.

Conversion

Converſion is nothing elſe but the turning away from the creature to return unto God.

The ſoul being once converted, or turned to God, finds a very great facility to continue thus turned unto him: and the more it continues turned, the nearer it approacheth God, and cleaveth to him; and the nearer it approacheth God, the farther doth it neceſſarily withdraw from the creature which is oppoſite to God. So that hereby the ſoul is ſo powerfully confirmed in its converſion, that it becomes habitual, and as it were natural unto it. But you muſt know that this is not done by any violent working or exerciſe of the creature. The only exerciſe it can and ought to do on its part, is by the grace of God, to exert a ſtrong endeavour to turn and gather itſelf inward; after which there is nothing more to be done, but to remain thus turned towards God in a continual adherence unto him.

God has an attractive virtue; which draweth the soul always more and more strongly to himself, and in drawing it he purifies it; just as we see the sun drawing up a thick vapour to itself; it attracts it gradually, the vapour using no other endeavour, but to let itself be drawn by the sun; which the nearer it brings it to its self, the more it subtilises and purifies it. There is only this difference, that this vapour is not drawn freely, and followeth not voluntarily, as the soul doth.

This manner of introverting or turning inward, is most easy, and advanceth the soul not by constraint or violence, but by her most natural propension or bias to God, because he is our center of rest. The centre hath always a most
powerful

powerful attractive virtue; and the more eminent and spiritual the centre is, the more violent and impetuous is its attraction or magnetism, and the more difficult it is to stop it.

But besides the attractive virtue of the centre, there is also given to all the creatures a mighty strong propension to a re-union with their centre: hence the most spiritual and perfect have this inclination strongest in them. No sooner does a thing return towards its centre than it precipitates with an extreme swiftness into it, if so be that it be not stopt by some invincible impediment in the way. A stone in the air is no sooner let go, towards the earth, than by its own proper weight it tends to it as its centre. Just so is it with the water and fire, which unless they are hindred, run incessantl to their centre. And thus it is that the foul, by the ſtrong endeavour which it uſes to gather itſelf inward, being once turned into this propenſion to its center, falls gradually into its centre, without any other effort but the weight of its love; and the more it continues peaceable and calm, without its own motion, the more ſwiftly doth it advance, becauſe it gives the more place to this attractive and central virtue, to draw it ſtrongly unto itſelf.

We ought then to make the recollecting ourſelves the moſt inwardly that is poſſible, the chief concern, and not be troubled at the pain and difficulty which this exerciſe may give us; for that will be very ſoon recompenced by a wonderful concurrence on God's part, which will render it moſt eaſy; provided we be faithful, meekly and gently to call back our heart, by a little sweet and peaceful retreat, and by serene and tender affections, whenever it is withdrawn through distractions or outward business. When at any time the passions arise, a little retreat inwards unto God, who is there present, doth allay them with great facility: any other way of engaging with them does rather exasperate than quiet them.

Sect. XII.

Of the Prayer of God's simple presence.

THE soul that is faithful in exercising itself, as hath been said, in love and affection to its God, is all amazed when it feels how by little and little he gets the entire possession of it. His presence becometh

Method of Prayer. 53

becometh now so easy to the soul, that it can no more be without it; it has acquir'd a habit of this as well as prayer. The soul feels the calm and serenity prevailing upon it by degrees: the silence maketh up its whole prayer, and God giveth it an infus'd love, which is the beginning of an unspeakable happiness. O! were I permitted to proceed and declare the infinite degrees that follow! But here I must stop, since that I write only for beginners, waiting till God shall be pleas'd to bring forth what may be serviceable for all states.

It must suffice only to say, that then it is of great consequence to cease from all self-activity, that God alone may act in us. *Be still and acknowledge that I am God;* is what he adviseth us by *David.* Ps. 45. 10. But the creature is so fond of what it does itself, that it believes

lieves it doth nothing, if it do not feel, know and diſtinguiſh its own operation. It does not ſee that the ſwiftneſs of its motion hindereth it from perceiving its ſteps, and that God's operation becoming more ſtrong ſwalloweth up that of the creature; even as we ſee that the ſun as it ariſes, doth gradually ſwallow up all the light of the ſtars, which were very diſtinct before he appeared. It is not for want of light that we cannot then diſtinguiſh the ſtars, but the exceſs of light.

The caſe is the ſame here; the creature can't diſtinguiſh its own operation, becauſe a general and ſtrong light abſorbeth all its little diſtinct lights, and by his ſurpaſsing ſplendor and brightneſs makes them entirely diſappear. So that they who charge this ſort of prayer with idleneſs, are very much miſtaken: and 'tis for want of experience

ence that they say so. O did they but give themselves some little trouble to make tryal of it! they would in a very little time know it experimentally.

I tell you therefore that this abatement of self-activity proceeds not of want, but of abundance, as any that will make the experiment, will clearly perceive. He will know that it is not an unfruitful silence, occasioned through want, but a silence full, and unctuous proceeding from abundance.

Two sorts of persons are silent, the one because they have nothing to say; and the other, because they have too much. The case is the same in this degree of prayer we speak of. They are silent not for want; but thro' fulness and excess.

The water causes death to two persons in a very different manner. One

One dieth of thirst, and the other is drowned: one dieth thro' the want, and the other thro' the abundance of it. Even so here, it is the abundance that makes the operations to cease. Therefore 'tis of great importance in this degree for one to remain in as much silence as possibly he can.

An infant at the nurses breasts gives us a sensible demonstration of this. It begins to move its tender lips, that it may cause the milk to come; but when the milk cometh in abundance, it is content to swallow it down, without making any sensible motion: if it should make any, it would but prejudice itself by spilling the milk, and so be oblig'd to give over.

Just so at the beginning of prayer, we ought first of all to move the lips of our affection, but when the milk of grace doth flow, there is nothing by us to be done, but to
abide

abide in ftilnefs and repofe, gently fwallowing down what is given in; and when the milk ceafeth to come, to move again the affection a little, as the infant doth the lip. Should we do otherwife, we could not profit by the grace, which is here communicated to draw the foul into the repofe of love, and not to excite it to the multiplicity of its own motions.

But what becometh of this child that fwalloweth the milk fo gently and in peace, without moving or ftirring ? Who could believe that it was nourifhed by this manner ? And yet the more it fucks in peace, the more it thrives by the milk. What is it, I fay, that happeneth to this child ? Why, it falleth afleep in its mother's bofom : and likewife the foul that is quiet and peaceful in prayer, falleth oftentimes into a fpiritual (or inward) flumber,

ber, wherein all the faculties and powers thereof are silent, until they are prepared to enter into the substance of that which is given them transiently. You see how the soul is here led in a way that is wholly natural, without pain, without violence, without study, without artifice.

The inward ground is not a strong hold that is to be taken by canon and storm: 'tis a kingdom of peace which is gain'd only by love. And thus if any one will but sweetly follow this little train, in the foresaid manner, he shall quickly arrive at infused prayer. God does not require any thing that is extraordinary or too difficult; but on the contrary, a meerly simple and child-like way of proceeding doth please him best.

That which is greatest and most eminent in religion, is indeed the

easiest of all. This is also true in
natural things. Would you go to
sea? Then take boat upon a river,
and you shall get at it insensibly
and without trouble. Would you go
to God? Take this so very sweet
and easy way, and you shall short-
ly come at him, in a manner that
will even surprize you. O if you
would but make the trial! you would
soon be convinced that we have
told you but a very little of it; for
then your own experience would
go very far beyond all that we have
said. O! what are you afraid of?
Why don't you readily cast yourself into the arms of essential love,
who stretched them forth upon the
cross only that he might receive
you. What danger can there be to
trust God, and purely to resign
yourself to him? Ah! he will not
deceive you, unless it be in a very
agreeable manner, namely, by giving

ing you much more than you expect; whereas they who expect any thing from themselves, may come to hear that rebuke which God giveth them by the mouth of the prophet Isaiah ch. 57. 10. vulg *Thou haſt wearied thyſelf in the multiplicity of thy ways, and yet thou haſt never ſaid, let me reſt in peace.*

Sect. XIII.

Of Reſt before God.

THE ſoul being arrived hither hath no need of any other preparation for going to God but of its *Reſt.* For here it is that the preſence of God begins to be infus'd and almoſt continual all the day long, which is the great fruit of prayer, or rather the continuation of it. Here the ſoul enjoys in its inward ground an inestimable happiness: it finds that God is more in it than its self. It hath but one only thing to do that it may find him, which is to sink down into itself. So soon as it shuts its bodily eyes, it finds itself taken up into a state of prayer: it stands amazed at this infinite good, and there passes a conversation within it, which the outward man doth not interrupt. That may be said of this manner of prayer; which is spoken of wisdom; *Wisd.* 7. 11. *All good things are come along with it.* For the virtues flow sweetly into this soul, which likewise practiseth them after so easy a manner, that they seem natural to it. A seed or spirit of life, and a principle of fecundity, springeth up in her, which giveth it a facility to all that is good, and an insensibility to all that is evil. Let it therefore faithfully persist in this

state

state, and beware that it seek not after any other disposition whatsoever, but its simple rest: it has nothing to do, but to suffer itself to be filled with this divine effusion. This is the most perfect internal disposition of which a soul is capable for receiving the sacrament, or performing any other religious duty.

Sect. XIV.

Of the inward Silence.

THE Lord is in his holy temple, let all the earth keep silence before him Hab. 2. 20.

The reason why the inward silence is so necessary, is, because this is a proper disposition, and requisite for receiving into the soul the Word, which is the eternal and essential speech.

It is a well known truth, that in order to receive the outward word, we must give ear and hearken. The sense of hearing, is made for receiving the word, which is spoken or communicated to it. The hearing is a sense more passive than active; it receiveth, but doth not communicate. And because the internal essential Word, desireth to speak within the soul, and to communicate itself to, and revive and quicken it; it is absolutely necessary that the soul be attentive.

On this account it is, that there are so many places in scripture, which exhort us to hear God, and to be attentive to his voice. We might easily observe a great many of them, but 'twill be sufficient to mention these two or three. Isa. 51.

4. *Hearken unto me all ye that are my people, and give ear unto my voice O nation that I have chosen!* And again, chap. 46. 3. vulg. *Hearken unto me all ye whom I bear in my bosom, and whom I carry in my bowels!* Again, Pf. 45. 10. *Hearken, O my daughter! Consider, and incline thine ear, forget thy kindred and thy father's house, so shall the king greatly desire thy beauty.*

External silence is most necessary to improve and cultivate the internal; and indeed 'tis impossible to become inward or spiritual, without loving silence and retirement. God himself tells us so by the mouth of his prophet, Hof. 2. 14. vulg. *I will lead her into solitude, and there will I speak to her heart.* How can one be inwardly taken up with God, and yet be outwardly busied about a thousand trifles? This is certainly impossible.

When your weakness at any time has led you to be scatter'd and distracted abroad, you must make a little retreat or retire inwards, to which you must always be faithful, whensoever you are scatter'd and dissipated. It would signify but little to pray, and recollect ones self for half an hour or an hour, if we do not preserve the unction and spirit of prayer all the day long.

Sect. XV.

Of Confession and Self-Examination.

EXAMINATION ought always to go before confession, and they that would perform it aright, must lay themselves open before God, who will not be wanting to enlighten

lighten them, and make them to know the nature of their faults. But they muſt take care to examine themſelves in peace and tranquility, expecting to have the knowledge of their ſins given them *from God*, rather than from their own particular ſcrutiny.

When we exert any ſtrong endeavours in examining ourſelves, we are readily miſtaken: we believe *the good to be evil, and the evil good*, Iſa. v. 20. and ſelf-love naturally deceives us. But when we expoſe ourſelves before the all-ſeeing God, this divine ſun diſcovers to us even the minuteſt actions Therefore we ought to abandon and reſign ourſelves to God, both as to examination and confeſſion.

So ſoon as the ſoul is advanced to this manner of prayer, God takes particular care to reprove it

fo

or all the faults it commits. It is
␣o sooner guilty of any escape or
␣eviation, but it feels a certain burn-
␣ng that rebukes it. Then it is that
␣God makes so strict an enquiry, that
␣␣e does not suffer any thing to es-
␣ape; and then the soul has no-
␣␣ing to do but to turn itself simply
␣owards God, and to suffer the
␣ain and correction which he in-
␣icteth.

Now this examination on God's
␣art being continual, the soul can-
␣ot any more examine itself: and
␣f it be faithful in resigning itself to
␣God, it will be much better tried
␣␣nd inspected into by his divine
␣ight, than it can be by all its own
␣ares; and experience will con-
␣␣ince it that this is true.

You must necessarily take notice
␣f one thing; *namely*, that the souls
␣vhich walk in this way will be often
␣urprized to find, that when they
begin

begin to confess their sins unto God, instead of sorrow and contrition, which they were wont to feel, a sweet and serene love seizes their heart. Those who are not acquainted with this matter would, it may be, withdraw from it to form an act of contrition, because they have heard say, that this is necessary. But they don't perceive that they lose the true contrition, which is this infused love, infinitely more important than any thing they could do of themselves. They have here one eminent act which comprehends the other acts with more perfection, though they have not these distinct and multiplied as before. Therefore let them not give themselves the trouble to do any other thing, when God acteth thus graciously in them, and with them.

To hate sin in this manner, is to
hate

late it as God doth. The pureſt love of any, is, that which God operates in the ſoul. Let it not therefore be eager to act, but let it remain ſuch as it is, according to the wiſe man's counſel, Eccluſ. xi. 22. *Put your truſt in God, and continue in reſt in the place where he hath ſet you.*

The ſoul will admire alſo that it ſhould forget its defects and failures, and have ſuch difficulty to remember them: yet it ought not to be troubled at this, for theſe two reaſons: one is, becauſe this forgetfulneſs is a ſign of its purification from the fault; and the excellency of this ſtate conſiſteth in this; *namely*, to forget all that concerneth us, that we may remember *God* only. The other reaſon is, that God faileth not to diſcover to the ſoul its greateſt faults: for he

he maketh the infpection himfelf
and the foul will fee, that by
this way it fhall better compaſ
its end, than by all its own en
deavours.

This is not to be applied to thoſe
ſtates, where the foul being yet in
the active part, may and ought to
ufe its care and induſtry in per
forming all things, more or lefs
according to the meafure of its ad
vancement. But as to the foul
that are come up to this degree, let
them keep to what we have told
them, and let them not change their
fimple and filent exercifes. Let
them fuffer God to act, and let
them keep filence.

Sect. XVI.

Of Reading, and of Vocal Prayers.

THE manner of reading in this degree is, that as soon as one [feel]s a little recollection of mind, [he] ought to cease, and remain in [stil]lness, reading but little, and not [go]ing on after he finds himself [dr]awn into the inward. The soul [is] no sooner call'd to internal si[len]ce, but it ought to forbear to [bu]rthen itself with vocal prayers, [ex]cept a very few; and even in [tho]se if it finds any difficulty, and [fee]ls itself drawn to silence, it should [ab]ide silent, and not strive or use [an]y effort against it.

Let it not vex itself, nor fetter [its]elf, but suffer itself to be led by

the

the Spirit of *God*, who will assured[ly]
lead it into all truth.

Sect. XVII.

Of Petitions.

HERE the soul will find itse[lf]
unable to make those re[-]
quests to God, which at other time[s]
it was wont to do with great facility[.]
But it ought not to be surprized a[t]
this; for then is it that the spir[it]
asketh for the saints that which [is]
good, and perfect, and agreeabl[e]
to the will of God: *The Spirit ass[ists]
us even in our infirmities, because w[e]
know not what to pray for as we ough[t,]
nor how to pray; but the Spirit itse[lf]
maketh intercession for us with groa[ns]
which cannot be uttered,* Rom. vii[i.]
26. Moreover, I say, we must f[

ond God's design, which is, chiefly, to strip the soul of its own operations, that he may substitute his in their room. Suffer him then to do so, and do not tie yourself to any thing of yourself, how good soever it may seem to be: for to be sure it is not then such to you, if it turns you away from that which God desireth of you; but the will of God is preferable to every other good besides. Rid yourself therefore of your own interests, and live by faith and resignation: here it is that faith begins to operate in the soul by way of eminency.

Sect. XVIII.

Of Defects or Infirmities

WHensoever we have fallen into any defect, or have at any time gone out of our way, we must immediately turn inwards; because this default having led us away from *God*, we ought as soon as possible to return unto him, and suffer patiently the compunction which he worketh in us.

It is a matter of great importance not to be vexed or disturbed because of our defects; for this trouble or disquiet proceedeth from a secret pride, or from the love and esteem of our own excellence. We are uneasy when we feel what we are: but if we despond or discourage ourselves thereby, we are weakened so much the more; and the reflection we make upon our faults begetteth in us a peevishness or fretting, which is worse than the fault itself.*

A soul that is truly humble doth not at all wonder at its infirmities; and the more it seeth itself miserable, the more it resigneth itself to *God,* and endeavoureth to keep close to him, seeing the great need that it hath of his assistance. We ought to observe this conduct so much the more, that God himself hath told it us, saying, *I will make thee to understand what thou oughtest to do;*

---

* *Trouble and disquiet do but sink and entangle the soul the more; whereas a vigorous act of conversion to the* divine presence *within us, attended with a lively faith and an humble confidence, doth infallibly extinguish the temptation, dispel the darkness, and overcome the enemy. And one that stands in God's presence must needs hate sin, as God hateth it.*

I will teach thee the way by which thou shouldst go, and I will have my eye continually upon thee for thy guide, Psa. xxxii. 8.

Sect. XIX.

Of Distractions and Temptations.

IN all our distractions and temptations, instead of combating them directly, (which would only encrease them, and take the soul off from adhering to God, which ought to be its continual employment) we ought simply to turn away our eye from them, and draw nearer and nearer to God; like a little child, which seeing a monster, doth not stand to fight him, nor yet so much as to look at him, but meekly sinketh down into its mother's bosom,

bosom, where 'tis safe and secure. *God is in the midst of her, she shall not be moved: he will help her, and that right early.* Psa. lxvi. 5.

When we poor feeble creatures do otherwise, thinking to attack our enemies, we find ourselves often wounded if not entirely defeated: but continuing simply in the presence of God, we shall soon find ourselves more than conquerors. This was *David's* conduct, *I have,* said he, *the Lord always present with me, and I shall not be moved: therefore my heart rejoiceth, and my flesh also shall rest in safety,* Psa. xvi. 8. Again 'tis said in Exodus xiv. 14. *The Lord shall fight for you, and you shall keep yourselves in peace.*

Sect. XX.

Of true Prayer and Adoration.

PRAYER, according to St John's account of it, is an incense, whose sweet smelling favour ascends to God: for which purpose *the angel held a censer, in which was the perfume of the prayers of the saints,* Rev. viii. 3.

Prayer is the pouring out of the heart in the presence of God: thus said *Samuel's* mother, *I have poured out my heart in the presence of the Lord,* 1 Sam. i. 15. Therefore the prayer which the kings or wise men poured forth at the feet of the child *Jesus,* in the stable of *Bethlehem* was signified by the incense which they offered. Prayer is nothing else but a warmth of love, which as it melts and diffolves the foul, fubtilizes it, and caufes it to afcend even to God: according as it is melted, fo it gives forth its fweet fmell, and this fmell cometh from the love which burneth it.

This the fpoufe meaneth when fhe faith, *While my Beloved was on his couch, my fpikenard fent forth the fmell thereof,* Cant. i. 12. The couch is the ground or centre of the foul: while God is there, and one knows how to dwell with him, and keep in his prefence, this prefence gradually melts and diffolves the hardnefs of this foul, and being melted it fends forths its *odours.* And therefore the Beloved, feeing that *his fpoufe was thus melted fo foon as he had fpoken,* Cant. v. 6. faith to her, *Who is this that afcendeth out of the wildernefs as a little cloud of perfume?* chap. iii. 6.

Thus doth this foul afcend to her God.

God. But to this end it muſt ſuffer *ſelf* or her *own will*, to be deſtroyed by the power of divine love. This is a ſtate of ſacrifice eſſential to the Chriſtian religion, whereby the ſoul ſuffereth the deſtruction of its *own will*, that the will of God may be done, and thereby rendereth true homage to the ſovereign of the univerſe; as 'tis written, *God alone is great, and he is honoured only by the humble*, Eccluſ. iii. 20. We muſt die to *ſelf* or our *own will*, that Jeſus Chriſt, who is *the Word* that liveth and abideth for ever, may live and prevail, be heard and obeyed. That our *own will*, or the life of *ſelf* being *dead, our life may be hid* with *Chriſt in God*. In which conſiſteth that adoration that giveth all *honour, glory*, and *power, unto God* and *our Redeemer for ever and ever*.

This is the prayer of truth; this is *to worſhip the Father in ſpirit and in truth*:

truth: John iv. 23. In *spirit*, because we are thereby drawn from our human and carnal manner of acting, to enter into the purity of the spirit which prayeth in us. And *in truth*, because the soul is thereby placed in the truth of the ALL of GOD, and of the NOTHING of *the creature*.

There are only these two truths, the *All* and the *Nothing*: every thing else is a counterfeit. We cannot honour *God's All*, but by our own *annihilation*; and we are no sooner annihilated, that is, emptied of ourselves; than *God*, who allows not any thing to be void without filling it, doth replenish us with himself.

O did we but know the infinite good which accrue to the soul from this prayer, we would scarce do any thing else! This is *the pearl of great price:* this is *the hidden treasure,*

sure. Mat. xiii. 44, 45. He that findeth it, most cheerfully selleth al that he hath to purchase it. This i *the river of living water, rising up unt eternal life.* John iv. 14, & 23. Th is to worship God in spirit and in truth and this is to practise the pure precepts of the gospel.

Doth not *Jesus Christ* assure us, Lu xvii. 21. that *the kingdom of God is with in us?* This kingdom is understoo two ways. One is, when God is f much master of us, that nothin doth any more resist him: then ou soul is truly his kingdom. Th other is, when possessing God wh is the sovereign good, we posse the kingdom of God, which is th height of felicity, and the very en for which we were created; according to the proverb, it tis said, *serve God is to reign.* The end fo which we were created is, to en joy God even in this life: ye

Method of Prayer. 83

as, this is least in the thoughts of
most men.

Sect. XXI.

That the soul acteth more disinterested and more nobly by this manner of prayer than by any other.

WHEN some persons hear of the prayer of silence, they groundlesly imagine, that therein the soul is placed in a state of stupidity, lifeless, and without action. But certain it is that there the soul acteth more nobly and with more enlargement, than ever it did hitherto; because in this kind of prayer it tis moved by *God* himself, and it acteth by his spirit. St. Paul would have us suffer ourselves *to be led by the spirit of God. Rom.* viii. 14.

We don't say, that the soul ought
not

not to act at all, but only that it ought to act dependently on the movement of grace. This is admirably described in the prophet *Ezekiel*'s vision of the wheels, *Chap*. i. 15 21. *The Wheels*, which he saw, *had the spirit of life, and they went whithersoever that spirit led them; they were lifted up or stood still, according as they were moved, for the spirit of life was in them; but they never returned back.* Thus ought it to be with the soul; it should suffer itself to be moved and led by the quickening spirit that is in it, following still the movement of its action, and never following any other. But this motion never inclines it to go back; that is, either to reflect upon the creature, or to bend towards itself; but to go always streight forward, advancing continually towards its end.

This action of the soul is an action

ion altogether quiet and serene. When it acteth by itself, it acteth with hurry and fatigue; and hereby it distinguisheth its own action. But when it acteth dependently on the spirit of grace, its action is so free, so easy, and so natural; that it seemeth as tho' it did nothing. *He hath brought me forth into a large place, he hath delivered me because he loved me.* Psal. xviii. 19.

So soon as the soul hath got into its central bent and tendency, that is to say, returned within itself by recollection, from that instant it begins to run its course towards its centre, the attractions of which give it at once the greatest vigor and the swiftest motion; for no swiftness is equal to that of its central tendency. This then is an action, but, it is so noble, so quiet, and so peaceable, that it seemeth to the soul

as tho' it doth not act at all, becauſ
its operation is ſo natural.

While a wheel is ſlowly turned, 'ti
eaſy to perceive its motion diſtinct
ly, but when it goeth very ſwiftly, w
can no longer diſtinguiſh any thin
in it; juſt ſo the ſoul which con
tinueth before God in quietneſ
hath an infinitely noble and elevat
ed action, but withal an action tha
is moſt peaceable. The more th
ſoul is in peace, the more ſwiftly i
runneth; becauſe it is wholly reſign
ed to that ſpirit which moveth i
and maketh it act.

This ſpirit is no other than Go
himſelf, who draweth us, and draw
ing us maketh us to run unto him
as the divine lover well knew whe
ſhe ſaid, Cant. i. 4. vulg. *Draw m*
and we will run. Draw me, O m
divine centre, by the profounde
deep of my being, and by this th
attraction the powers and ſenſ
ſha

shall all run to thee! This attraction then is both an ointment which healeth, and a perfume which draweth us; *we will run* faith she, *because of the smell of thy perfumes*: this is a most powerful attractive virtue, yet a virtue which the soul follows most freely, and which being equally strong and sweet, both draws by its power and charms by its sweetness. *Draw me* (faith the spouse) *and we will run*. She speaketh of herself and to herself. *Draw me*, behold the unity of the centre which attracts; *we will run*, behold the running and correspondence of all the powers and senses, which follow the attraction of the inward ground of the soul.

Therefore we don't in the least affirm that we ought to remain idle, but that we ought to act only in dependance on the spirit of *God*, which should animate us, since 'tis only

only *in him, and by him, that we live that we act, and that we are, Acts* xvii 28. This meek dependance upon the spirit of God, is abosutely necessary, and the soul will thereby infallibly arrive to that simplicity and unity in which it was at first created and it will thereby attain the end of its creation. Therefore we must quit the multiplicity of our actions, that we may enter into the simplicity and unity of God, *in whose image we were created. Gen.* i. 27. *The spirit of God is one only and manifold* or multiplied, Wisd. vii. 22. yet his unity hindereth not at all his multiplicity. We enter into his unity when we are united to his spirit, as having thereby one and the same spirit with him : and without departing from this unity, we are multiplied outwardly, in what regardeth his will. So that God acting infinitely and we suffering ourselves to b led by his spirit, go much further than our utmost activity could carry us.

We must suffer ourselves to be guided by the eternal wisdom: *For this wisdom is more moving or active than the most moveable things, Wis.* ch. 7. 24. Let us then abide in dependance upon his motions, and we shall act indeed most powerfully. *By the Word were all things made, and without him was not any thing made that was made.* Joh. i. 3. God created us at first after his own image and likeness, and he inspireth into us the spirit of the *Word, by that breath of life, Gen.* ii. 7, which he gave us when we were form'd to God's image, by the participation of this life of the Word, who is the image of his father: now this life is one, simple, pure, intimate and always fruitful. The devil having spoiled and disfigured this beautiful

image

image by sin, it was necessary that the same Word, whose spirit was breathed into us at our creation, should come to repair it. It was needful it should be done by him, because he is the essential image of his Father, and the defaced image does not repair itself by acting, but in being passive to the action of him who came to repair it.

Our action therefore ought only to be, to put ourselves in a condition to suffer God's acting upon us, and to give place unto the Word, to new model again his image in us. An image that should always be in motion, would hinder the painter from drawing any design upon it. All the motions which we make by our own spirit, do hinder this admirable painter from exactly working, and do occasion the making imperfect strokes. We must therefore remain in peace,
not

not moving ourfelves but when he moveth us. *Jefus Chrift hath the life in himfelf,* Joh. v. 26. and every one that would live muft receive life from him.

That this motion is the more noble, is a matter without difpute, for certainly things have no value or worth, but fo far as the principle whence they proceed is noble and fublime, and the actions of a divine principle are divine actions; whereas the actions of the creature, how good foever they feem to be, are but human, or at the very beft, but moral virtues. Jefus Chrift faith, that he hath the life in himfelf: all other beings have nothing but a borrowed life, but the Word hath the life in himfelf; and being communicative of his nature, he defireth to communicate of his life to men. Therefore we muft give way to this life,
that

that it may flow into us; which cannot be done but by the emptying ourselves, and loosing of the life of Adam, and our own will, as St. Paul assures us, 1 Cor. v. 17. *If any one be in Christ Jesus, he is a new creature: all that was old is done away; all is become new.* Which cannot be done but by the death of our own self-activity, to the end that God may act in us, and his divine will may be substituted in the place of ours.

It is not therefore pretended, that men should not act at all; but only that all our doings should be in dependance on being guided by the Spirit of God, giving way to his action in lieu of that of the creature. Which cannot be done but by consent of the creature, and the creature cannot give this consent, but by moderating its own activity, to give way by little and little that God's

God's operation may succeed in its stead.

Jesus Christ in the gospel, teaches us this is the way: *Martha* did good things, but because she did them in her own spirit, he reproved her. The spirit of man is turbulent and unquiet, and therefore it doth but little, though it appears to do a great deal. *Martha, Martha,* said *Christ*. Luke x. 41, 42. *you disquiet and torment yourself with a great many things; but after all, there is but one thing needful.* Mary *hath chosen the better part, which shall not be taken from her.*

What hath Mary chosen? It is peace, tranquillity, and rest. She ceaseth to act in appearance, that she may suffer herself to be moved by the spirit of *Jesus Christ*; she ceaseth to live, that so *Jesus Christ* may live in her: and therefore it is so very necessary to renounce

renounce ones self and ones own operations, if we would follow *Jesus Christ:* for we can never follow *Jesus Christ* unless we are animated with his spirit. Now that the Spirit of *Christ* may be brought forth in us, it is necessary that our own spirit give place unto him. *Whosoever doth cleave or adhere to the Lord,* (faith St. *Paul,* 1 Cor. vi. 17.) *becometh one spirit with him.* And *David* said, Pf. lxxiii. 28. vulg. that *It was good for him to adhere unto God, and to put his whole confidence in him.* What is this adhesion? It is a beginning of union with Christ.

In this union there is a beginning, continuation, finishing, and perfect consummation. The beginning or entering into our union, is an inclination of the soul towards God. When the soul is introverted or turned inwards, in the manner aforesaid, it is in a tendency
to

to its centre, and hath a ſtrong propenſion to union. In this propenſion is the union begun. Afterwards when it approacheth nearer to God, it adhereth, then it is united with him; and thence forwards becometh one ſpirit with him. Then it is that this ſpirit, which went forth from God, returns back unto God; it hath attained the end of its creation.

This divine life, this Spirit of Jeſus Chriſt, is the way we muſt of neceſſity walk in, for St. *Paul* aſſures us that *no man is Jeſus Chriſt's, if he hath not* his *Spirit.* Rom. viii. 9. Now then that we may be one with Chriſt, we muſt ſuffer ourſelves to be emptied of our own, that ſo we may be filled with his ſpirit; which we cannot be ſo long as we are full of ourſelves. St. Paul in the ſame place, Ver. 14. further proves the **neceſſity of** our being

thus

thus moved by this bleſſed ſpirit when he ſaith, *All they that are acted by the ſpirit of God, are the children o God.* The ſpirit of the divine filiation, is therefore that of the divine nature animating us: therefore the apoſtle adds, *The ſpirit which ye hav received is not a ſpirit of ſervitude to mak you live in fear: but it is the ſpirit o God's children, whereby we cry, Abba Father!*

By no other ſpirit than that o *Chriſt*, can we partake of his filiation or ſonſhip; and *this ſpirit dot itſelf bear witneſs to ours, that we ar the children of God,* Rom. viii. 16 So no ſooner doth the ſoul leave and give up itſelf to be animated by the ſpirit of God, but it experienceth in itſelf the teſtimony o this divine filiation: and this teſti mony greatly encreaſeth its joy, b the clear evidences it gives th ſoul, that *it is called to the liberty o God*

God's children, and that the spirit which it hath received, is not a spirit of servitude, but of liberty. The soul then feels that it acteth freely and sweetly, though strongly and infallibly.

St. Paul proves from our ignorances concerning the things we pray for, the necessity of our being in all things conducted, moved and animated by this divine Spirit: *The spirit*, saith he, *helpeth our infirmities; for we know not what to pray for, nor how to pray as we ought: but the spirit itself prayeth for us with groanings which are unutterable.* This is certain; if we do not know what we want, nor yet how to pray as we ought, for those things which are necessary for us; and if the spirit that is in us, to whose motion we give up ourselves, must needs ask and pray for us, ought we not then to let this spirit do it? This spirit is the spirit of the Wor[d] whose petition is always heard an[d] granted, as he said himself; *I kno[w] that thou hearest me always*, John x[i.] 42. Did we let this spirit pray an[d] interceed in us, we should alway[s] have our petitions heard an[d] granted. And why so ? It is (add[-] eth St. *Paul*) *because he that searche[s] the hearts, knows what the spirit desi[r-] eth, forasmuch as he intercedeth a[c-] cording to God for the saints*, Rom[.] viii. 27. That is to say, becau[se] this spirit asketh for that only whic[h] is conformable to the will of Go[d.] The will of God is, that we shoul[d] be saved, and that we should b[e] perfect. He therefore asks, or in[-] terceeds for that which is necessar[y] for our perfection.

Why then after all this, do w[e] oppress ourselves with superfluo[us] cares, and weary out our lives i[n] the multiplicity of our own way[s] withou[t] without ever saying, *Let us rest in peace?* God himself inviteth us to rest from all our labours and disquiets, and to stay ourselves on him: nay, he complaineth in the prophet *Isaiah*, chap. lv. 2. with an inconceivable goodness, that we employ the soul's strength, its riches and its treasure, in a thousand outward things, seeing that there is so very little to be done that we may enjoy the infinite good things which we propose to ourselves. *Wherefore do ye spend your money for that which cannot nourish you? and your labour for that which cannot satisfy you? Hearken unto me attentively, feed yourselves with the good nourishment which I do give you: and your souls being made fat therewith, shall indeed rejoice.*

O that men did but know what happiness it is to hearken unto

God in this manner, and how exceedingly the soul is thereby strengthened! *All flesh must needs be silent in the presence of the Lord*, Zac. ii. 13. All must cease and be still so soon as he appeareth. Now God, to oblige us yet further to abandon ourselves without any reserve, assureth us by his prophet, that we need not be afraid of any thing in giving up ourselves to him; because he taketh care of every one in particular. *Can a mother forget her own child,* (saith God) *and have no compassion on the son whom she hath conceived in her bowels? But even though she should forget, yet will not I ever forget you,* Isa. xlix. 15. O blessed words! full of divine consolation! who will any longer be afraid to surrender himself entirely to the guidance of God?

SECT.

Sect. XXII.

Of Internal Acts.

THE acts of man are either external or internal. The external are those that appear outwardly with regard to some sensible object, and which have no other moral good or evil, but what they receive from the internal principle whence they proceed.

I do not intend to speak then, but of internal acts of the soul, only whereby it inwardly holds to some object, and so forsakes another. For instance, if when any soul is applied to *God*, I will do some act of another nature, I thereby forsake *God*, so much as the act of my turning toward created things is stronger

stronger or weaker: on the other hand, if when my soul is turned towards the creature, I will return to God, there must be an act to withdraw my soul from the creature and to turn it to *God*: and by how much the more perfect this act is, by so much the more entire is the conversion. But till I am perfectly converted, I am continually under a necessity of making acts of turning to God, (this may be accomplished by some at once, which others do by little and little,) however, in each act I ought to exert the whole strength of my soul to return to God, according to the counsel of the Son of *Syrach*, *Re-unite all the motions of thy heart in the holiness of God*, chap. xxx. 24. And as *David* did, *I will keep my whole strength for thee*; Psa. lviii. 10. which is done by entering strongly into ones self; as faith the scripture, *Return to your heart,* Isaiah xlvi. 8. for we have wandered from our heart by sin; and therefore God demands but our heart, saying, *My son give me thy heart, and let thine eyes be always fixed upon my ways,* Prov. xxiii. 26. To give ones heart to God, is to have at all times the eye, the force and vigor of the soul fixed upon him, and cleaving unto him, that one may perfectly follow his will in all things. Wherefore, when the heart is once applied to God, it ought to continue thus turned towards him.

But the mind of man being frail and full of levity, and the soul accustomed to roam abroad, is easily diverted and dissipated; and therefore so soon as it perceives itself wandering abroad amongst outward things, it must, by a simple act, return towards God,

God, and reinstate itself in him: then its act will subsist so long as its conversion lasteth, by the powerful influence of its simple and unfeigned return to God. We know actions often repeated make a custom, so that by this means the soul will be accustomed to conversion, and this custom continued makes the action become altogether natural and habitual.

And then the soul ought not to perplex itself in seeking to form this act, because it is already formed and subsists; nay, it cannot do it, without finding very great difficulty in it: besides it will find that hereby it is drawn from its proper state, under pretence of seeking after it, which is a thing it should never do; especially since the act subsists, and the soul is then in an habitual conversion and in an habitual love. Men

Men feek after one act by feveral other acts, inftead of keeping themfelves fixed by a fimple act to *God* alone.

One may obferve, that fometimes he can with great eafe make fuch acts diftinctly, but fimply; which is a fign that he was gone aftray, and that now he enters again into his heart, after he had wandered from it. But let him take care to remain there in peace, now that he is returned to it. When any one thinks that he ought not to form any acts, he is much miftaken, for he forms always fome acts: but every one ought to form them according to the degree he is advanced to.

To clear up this place fully, which is indeed fome difficulty, (the greateft part of fpiritual perfons, not comprehending it,) you

you must know that some acts are transient and distinct, and others are continued; again, some acts are direct, and others reflex. All cannot form the first, neither are all in the proper state of forming the second. The first sort of acts ought to be made by the persons who are gone astray: they ought to turn themselves again by an act which they distinguish, and which should be more or less strong, according as the diversion or turning aside was greater or smaller; so that when the straying is but little, one of the most simple acts is sufficient.

I call that the *continued act*, by which the soul is wholly turned towards its God by a direct act, which is not renewed by it, unless interrupted, because the first remains entire. The soul, I say,

being

being turned after this manner, is indeed in the *love*, and dwelleth therein. *And he who dwelleth in love, dwelleth in God,* 1 John iv. 16. Then the soul hath entered as it were into the habit of the act, in which it reposeth: yet its repose is not idle; for the first act continues all the while, which is a sweet retirement into God, to which God attracteth it always most strongly; and the soul so readily following this powerful attraction, and abiding in his love, is always more and more ingulfed and swallowed up in love; and here its action is infinitely more strong, and more vigorous, than the first act which served for nothing but to bring it home from its wandering.

Now the soul in this profound and

and strong act, being wholly turned towards its God, hath not any perception of this act, because it is direct and not reflex. Which is the reason that this person not explaining himself well, saith, that he does not form any acts: but it is a mistake, for he never did any either better or more active. Let him rather say, I do not now distinguish any acts: and not I do not do any acts. 'Tis true he doth not do them by himself, but he is drawn, and he followeth that which draweth him. *Love* is the weight which sinketh him down, as a person falling into the sea sinketh, and would sink even to infinity, if the sea were infinite: and without his perception of it, he would descend into the lowest deep, with an incredible swiftness.

Therefore to say, that one doth no acts, is to speak improperly. All do acts, but all do them not after the same manner; and further the mistake cometh hence, that many who know they must do acts, would do them distinct and sensible. Which indeed cannot be; for the sensible ones are for beginners, and the others are for advanced souls. To stop in the first acts, which are weak, and advance but little, is to deprive ones self of the last. So in like manner, to endeavour to do the last acts without having passed through the first, were another no less considerable error.

All things then ought to be done in their proper season. Every state hath its *beginning*, its *progress*, and its *end*. He would be very wrong that should resolve not to go further than the beginning or first
stage.

stage, but fix himself there. There is no art which hath not its progress At the beginning there must be labouring with diligence and toil but then there follows an enjoying the fruit of ones labour. When ship is in the dock, the mariners are forced to take pains to launch her thence into the main ocean but afterwards they easily turn her to any coast they would steer. In like manner, while the soul is yet in sin and in the creatures, there much struggling and toil required to draw it out thence; there must be an untying or breaking of the cords which hold it bound; by means of strong and vigorous acts, with endeavours to draw the soul inward, removing it by little and little from its own port, and in removing from thence, turn it inwards God, which is the haven whereunto we desire to sail.

When the vessel is turned after this manner, proportionably as he advanceth in the sea, she is at distance from the land: and the further she is from the land, the less need is there of any labour to draw her along. At last they begin to sail most pleasantly, and the vessel runs so forcibly that they must quit the oars, which are now become useless. What doth the pilot then? He contenteth himself to spread the sails, and hold the rudder. To spread the sails, is to make the prayer of simply exposing or laying ones self open before God, in order to be moved by his spirit. To hold the rudder, is to keep our heart from wandering out of the right path, recalling it gently, and guiding it according to the motion of the spirit of God, which by degrees getteth possession of the heart, even as the wind cometh by little

little and little to fill the sails and drive on the veſſel. So long as the ſhip hath the wind fair, the pilot and mariners ceaſe from their labour, and repoſe themſelves what a progreſs do they now make without fatiguing themſelves? They make more way in one hour in repoſing themſelves after this manner, and leaving the veſſel to the conduct of the wind, than they could do in a great deal of time by all their firſt utmoſt efforts; and if they would then row, beſides greatly fatiguing themſelves, their labour would be quite uſeleſs, and they would retard the veſſel.

This is the very conduct which we ought to obſerve in the ſpiritual life, and by acting in this manner we ſhall advance more in a little time by being moved by the divine ſpirit, than we can any other way by a great many of our own ſtruggl-
ing

ings and efforts. Would people but take this method, they should find it the easiest in the world.

When the wind is contrary and the storm great, the anchor must be cast into the sea, to stop the vessel. This anchor is nothing else but confidence in God, and hope in his goodness, waiting in patience for the calm, and for fair weather, and till the wind prove favourable again; as did *David*: *I have waited* (saith he) *Pf.* 40. 1. *for the Lord with great patience, and he hath at last humbled himself even to me.* We must therefore give up and resign ourselves to the spirit of God, leaving ourselves to be guided by his motions.

Sect. XXIII.

An admonition to Pastors and Preachers.

IF all those that labour to gain souls, did endeavour to win them by the heart, putting them immediately upon prayer, and into the inward life, they would make numberless and lasting conversions. But so long as they go the other way to work, namely, by that which is external; and that instead of drawing souls to Jesus Christ, by the occupation of the heart in him, they do only load them with a thousand precepts for outward exercises; there comes but very little fruit thereof, and even that little does not endure.

 If ministers would zealously instruct

instruct their parishoners after this manner, the very shepherds in keeping their flocks, might have the spirit of the primitive Christians; and the ploughmen in guiding their plough-share, might entertain themselves in a blessed intercourse with God: the tradesmen and labourers that are spending themselves with toil, might gather from hence everlasting fruits: wickedness might be banished in a little time, and the whole parish become spiritual.

For when once the heart is won, all the rest is easily corrected. Thence it is that God principally demands the heart. By this method alone, drunkenness, blasphemy, uncleanness, animosity, theft, and the whole train of evils, which do so universally prevail, might be quite destroyed. Christ might reign peaceably over all, and the
appearance

appearance of his church might be seen once again in every place. Errors in the fundamentals of Chriftianity, are entered into the world, through the lofs of the life of God in the foul: if this were eftablifhed again, thofe errors would foon be deftroyed. That error gets the poffeffion of fouls, 'tis through want of faith and of prayer; if we taught our wandering brethren to believe fimply, and to pray, inftead of much difputing with them, we might bring them back gently to God.

O what ineftimable loffes are fuftained by the neglect of this fimple inftruction! O what account have thofe perfons that have the charge of fouls to give to God, for not having difcovered this hidden treafure, to all them whom they ferve by the miniftry of the word!

They excufe themfelves under the

the pretence, that there is danger in this way, or that common people are incapable of the things of the spirit. But the oracle of truth assures us of the contrary, saying, Prov. xii. 22, *The Lord placeth his affection on those who walk in simplicity.* And what danger can there be to walk in the one only way, which is *Jesus Christ*, giving ourselves entirely to him, beholding him continually, putting our whole confidence in his grace, and tending with all our strength and might to his pure love?

So far is it from being true, that the simple, the plain and the ignorant, are incapable of this essential accomplishment, that they are indeed the more fit for it; because they are more teachable, more humble, and more innocent; and because not being used to reasoning, they do not so much adhere
to

to their own judgments: being moreover without knowledge, they let themselves be moved and acted more easily by the spirit of God; whereas others, who are tied down and blinded by their own self-sufficiency, do resist a great deal more the divine inspiration. Thus God declareth to us, that 'tis to the little ones that he gives the understanding of his law: *The entrance of thy word* (saith *David*) Pf. cxix. 130. *giveth light, it giveth understanding to the simple.* He assureth us likewise, Prov. iii. 32. that he loveth *to converse familiarly with the simple ones. The Lord preserveth the simple; I was reduced to extremity, and he saved me.* Pf. cxvi. 6. Let pastors and teachers then take heed, not to hinder the little children from coming to *Christ. Suffer these little children* (said he to his apostles) Mat. xix. 14. *to come unto me; for it is*

Method of Prayer. 119

unto them that the kingdom of heaven doth belong. Jesus Christ said this to the apostles, because they would have hindered the children from coming unto him. Oftentimes men apply the remedy to the body, and mean while the disease is at the heart.

The great reason why their success in the reformation of men is so small and transient, especially of labouring persons, is, because ministers and teachers set about it outwardly. Did they but give them at first *the key to the hidden life of God in the soul,* Reformation of the outward actions would naturally follow. Now this is most easy, namely, to teach them to seek God in their hearts, to think upon him, to return unto him there, whenever they find themselves distracted, to do all things, and suffer all things with a design to please him:
this

this is to send them to the fountain of all good, and shewing them where to find all that is necessary for their sanctification and salvation.

I earnestly request and conjure all you who minister to souls, to put them immediately into the way, which is *Jesus Christ*; and he conjures you this, by all the blood which he hath shed for these souls whom he hath entrusted to your ministry: *Speak ye to the heart of Jerusalem,* Isaiah xl. 2. O ye preachers of his word! O ye ministers of his sacraments! Establish his kingdom; and that you may establish it truly, make him to reign over hearts! For as it is the heart alone which can oppose itself to his empire; so is it by the total subjection of the heart that his sovereignty is the most honoured. *Give ye glory to the holiness of God, and he shall become your sanctification,* Isa. viii. 13. Teach your people how to pray, not by reading forms of devotion, but by the prayer of the heart, and not of the head; a prayer of the spirit of God, and not of man's invention.

Alas! Men will be making studied prayers; and while they seek to adjust them too much, they render them impracticable. They have estranged the children from the best of all fathers, in teaching them a language too polite. Go ye, poor children, speak to your heavenly Father in your own language; how barbarous and rude soever it be, it is not so to him. A father loveth rather a discourse, which love and respect may put into disorder, (forasmuch as he seeth that this cometh from the heart) than an harangue that is dry, empty and barren, though
never

never so well studied. O how mightily do the glances of love in the heart delight and please him! They express infinitely more than all the fine language, whether of extempore, or of the best *invented* forms of prayer.

Men in endeavouring to teach how to love by rule and method, have in a great measure lost the love itself. O how little necessary it is to teach an art of loving! The language of love is barbarous to him who is not in love, but it is very natural to him that is in love: and one can never better learn how to love God, than in loving him. In this case the most dull become the most expert, because they behave themselves more simply and more cordially. The spirit of God hath no need of our regulations, he taketh up shepherds, when he pleaseth, to make

make of them prophets: and so far is he from shutting the palace of prayer against any one, as some imagine, that, on the contrary, he leaveth all the gates thereof open to all; and *wisdom* crieth in the public places, *Whoso is simple, let him come unto me*, Prov. ix. 4. And she saith unto them that are without understanding, *Come ye, eat of the bread which I give you, and drink of the wine, which I have prepared you*, ver. 3. Doth not Jesus Christ thank his Father, *That he hath hidden his secrets from the wise, and hath revealed them to the little ones*, Matt. xi. 25.

Sect. XXIV.

What is the safest Method to arrive at the Divine Union.

IT is impossible to arrive at the divine union by the way of meditation only, or even of the affections; or by any luminous and distinctly comprehended prayer whatsoever. There are several reasons for it: behold here the principal.

In the *first* place, according to the scripture, *No man shall see God so long as he is living*, Exod xxxiii. 20. Now all the exercise of discursive prayer, or even of active contemplation, (considered as an end, and not as a disposition to the passive) are living exercises,
whereby

Method of Prayer.

whereby we cannot see God; that is to say, be united to him. It is necessary, that whatever is of man, and of his own industry, how noble and exalted soever it may be; 'tis necessary, I say, that all this should die. St. *John* reports, that *in heaven there was a great silence*, Rev. viii. 1. Heaven represents the ground and the centre of the soul, where all must be in silence, while the majesty of *God* appears therein, all the efforts of our own strength, and all our own self-sufficiency must be destroyed; because nothing is opposite to God but selfishness; and all the malignity of man is in this principle of *self* subsisting, it being the source of his evil nature: so that the more any soul loseth its own will or selfish property. the more pure it becometh; and that which would be a defect in a soul living to itself,

self, is not so any more, by reason of the purity and innocence which it hath contracted, since it lost that which caused the unlikeness to its God.

Secondly, To unite two such contraries, as are the purity of God and the impurity of the creature; the simplicity of God, and the multiplicity of man, 'tis needful that God do singularly operate. For this can never be effected by the effort of the creature, since two things cannot be united which have no similarity or likeness to each other; even as an impure metal will never be fully united with gold that is solidly pure.

What doth God do in this case? He sendeth before him his own *wisdom,* even as the fire shall be sent upon the earth, to consume by its activity whatsoever is of impure therein. The fire consumeth

sumeth all things, and nothing resisteth its activity. It is the same with *wisdom*; it consumeth every impurity in the creature, to dispose it for the divine union.

This impurity, which is so opposite to divine union, is selfishness and activity. Selfishness, because it is the source of impurity, which can never be joined with essential purity: even as the rays of the sun may indeed touch the dirt, but cannot unite with it.

Activity, because God being in an infinite rest, 'tis necessary, in order to the soul being made capable of union with him, that it do partake of his rest; without which he cannot be united with it, by reason of the unlikeness: since that two things may be united, 'tis necessary that they be in a proportionable rest.

And it is for this reason that the soul

soul arriveth not to the divine union, but by the resting of its will; and it cannot be united unto God, until it be in a central rest, and in the purity of its creation. To purify the soul, God maketh use of *wisdom;* as fire is made use of to purify gold. It is certain that gold cannot be purified but by the fire, which consumes by little and little all that is earthly and of a contrary nature therein, and separates it from the gold. It is not enough for the gold, in order to be made use of by the goldsmith, that the earthly part be mixed with the gold: 'tis necessary moreover that the fire do melt it, for to draw out of its substance whatever remains in it that is of a contrary or earthly nature: and this gold is cast so often into the fire till it loseth all impurity, and every

every difpofition that is left to be purified.

When the goldfmith can find no more mixture, becaufe it is come to its perfect purity and fimplicity, the fire can no more act upon it; and it might be there an age, without being made thereby more pure, and without any the leaft diminution of its fubftance. Then it is fit for the moft excellent works; and if this gold contracts any impurities at any time afterwards, thefe are defilements newly contracted only by the commerce and nearnefs of foreign bodies. But there is this difference, that this impurity is merely fuperficial, and doth not make it unfit for ufe: whereas the other impurity was hidden in the centre or ground, and as it were interwoven with its nature. Neverthelefs perfons who are unacquainted with this, feeing

a piece

a piece of pure gold that is truly refined, covered outwardly over with filth, would not value it so much, as they would a piece of coarfe gold that is very impure when its outfide is polifhed.

Moreover, you may obferve that gold of an inferior degree of purity, cannot be joined with that of a fuperior degree of purity there is a neceffity for the one to contract of the impurity of the other, or for this to partake of the purity of that. To mix fine gold with coarfe, is what the goldfmith will never do. What will he then do? He will caufe all the earthly mixture of this impure gold to be deftroyed, by the fire, to the end he may be able to unite it with the purity of the firft. And this is i that St. *Paul* faith, namely, *that our works fhall be tried as by fire, that what is combuftible may be burnt*

1 Cor. iii. 13, 15. He addeth, *that the person whose works shall be found fewel for the fire shall be burnt although he himself shall be saved, yet so as by fire.* The meaning is, that there are certain works which are accepted and approved; but to the end that he who hath wrought them may be also pure, it is needful that they pass thro' the fire, that so the selfish mixture may be taken from them: and it is in this sense that God will examine and *judge our righteousnesses, Pf.* lxxv. 2. vulg. Because *man shall never be sanctified by the works of the law, but by the righteousness of the faith which cometh of God. Rom.* iii. 20.

This being once laid down, I say, that to the end man may be united to his God, there is a necessity that his *wisdom*, accompanied with the divine justice as a devouring fire, should extirpate and root out of the

the foul, all whatfoever it hath of earthly, carnal, and felf-activity; that having cleanfed and purified the foul from all this, God may unite himfelf to it. Which can never be done by the induftry of the creature: on the contrary, the creature fuffereth it even with regret: becaufe, as I have faid, man loveth fo ftrongly his own will, and dreadeth fo much its deftruction that if God did not do it himfelf, and with authority, man would never confent to it.

To this it may be anfwered me that God never taketh from man his liberty, and that thus he can always refift God: from whence i followeth, that I ought not to fay that God acteth abfolutely, and without the confent of man. Tha this may be done, and yet the en tire freedom and liberty of th will not be violated, I explain myfel myself and say, that it sufficeth then that man give a passive consent, because that having given up himself to God, at the beginning of his Christian course, that God might do with him and in him, whatever he would. he gave then an active and general consent to whatever *God* should do. But when God destroyeth, burneth, and purifieth, the soul seeth not that this is advantageous to it, but believeth rather the contrary; and even as the fire seemeth at first to foil the gold, so this operation seemeth to rob the soul of its purity. So that if an active and explicit consent were then needful, the soul would have difficulty to give it, and very often it would not give it at all. The most the soul doth, is to keep itself in a passive consent, suffering as well as it can this operation, which it neither *can* nor *will* hinder.

M Therefore

Therefore God purifieth in such wise the soul from all its own operations and the workings of self, which make it so very unlike him, that in fine he renders it by little and little, conformable to himself; exalting the passive capacity of the creature, enlarging it, and enobling it; though after an hidden and unknown manner, which is hence called mystical. But it is necessary that in all these operations the soul concur passively. It is true, that in the beginning before it cometh to this, it must be more active; and then, according as the divine operation groweth stronger, the soul must gradually and successively yield and give way unto God, until it be perfectly absorpt in him. But this is a long while effecting.

We do not then say (as some have believed) that there is no need to pafs through action; fince, on the contrary, this is the very gate: but only that one muft not always dwell there, feeing man ought to tend to the perfection of his end; but he can never arrive at it without quitting the firft helps and means; which, though neceffary to introduce him into this way, would greatly retard his progrefs, and if obftinately perfifted in would hinder him from arriving at his end. This is what St. Paul did: *I leave* (faith he) Phil. iii. 14. *that which is behind, and I endeavour to advance forward, that fo I may finifh my courfe.*

Would not they fay, that a perfon had loft his fenfes, if having undertaken a journey, he would ftop at the firft inn, becaufe he was certainly informed that feveral have paffed that way, that fome have lodged there, and that the mafter of the houfe dwells there? All that we wifh for then from people is, that they go on ftill towards their end; that they take the fhorteft and eafieft way; that they do not ftop at the firft place they come to; and that following the counfel of St. Paul, they leave themfelves to be moved and led by the fpirit of grace, who will conduct them to the end for which they were created, which is, to enjoy God.

None can be ignorant, that the fovereign good is *God*; that effential happinefs confifteth in the union with *God*; that the faints are more or lefs glorified, according as this union is more or lefs perfect and that this union cannot be made in the foul by any activity of its own, fince God does not communicate himfelf to the foul, but in proportion as its paffive capacity is enlarged. No one can be unit

Method of Prayer. 137

ed to God without paffiveneſs, and fimplicity; and this union being the beatitude itſelf, the way or method which conducts us into this paffiveneſs cannot be evil; on the contrary, it is preferable to all other.

This way is in no wiſe dangerous; if it were, would *Jeſus Chriſt* have made it the moſt perfect and the moſt neceſſary of all ways? All can walk in it; and as all are called to bleſſedneſs, all are alſo called to enjoy God both in this life and in the next; foraſmuch as the *enjoyment of God* conſtitutes our bleſſedneſs or happineſs. I ſay, of *God himſelf*, and not of his gifts; which could never make the eſſential bleſſedneſs, nor be capable of giving full contentment and ſatisfaction to the ſoul. For the ſoul is ſo noble and ſo magnificent, that all the gifts of God, even the greateſt,

eſt, could not render it happy, if God do not give himſelf unto it. Now God's whole deſire is to give himſelf unto his creature, according to the capacity which he hath placed in it: and yet, alas! Men are afraid to ſurrender themſelves to God! They are afraid to poſſeſs him, and to diſpoſe themſelves for the divine union.

Some ſay, that none ought to put themſelves into it of themſelves. I grant it. And I ſay alſo, that no creature can ever do this, ſince there is not a creature in the world that is able to unite itſelf to God by all its own efforts: it muſt be God that muſt unite it to himſelf. If therefore one cannot be united to God by ones ſelf, it is to cry out againſt a chimera, to cry out againſt them who put themſelves into it of themſelves.

Theſe will ſay, that ſome do feign

feign themselves to be in it. I say that this cannot be feigned; for he who dieth of hunger cannot feign, especially for a long time, that he is in perfect fulness. There will escape from him always some desire, or longing, by which he will soon discover that he is very far from his end.

Since therefore no man can enter into his end, except he be placed therein, our concern here is not to introduce any one into it, but to shew them the way which leadeth thither; and at the same time to beseech and conjure them, that they would not keep themselves tied up, and fixed to any means or exercises, which must be quitted when the signal is given; which is known and understood by the *experienced* teacher, who sheweth the living water, and endeavoureth to introduce into it. And would

would it not be a cruelty that deserves to be punished, to shew a spring to a thirsty man, but then to keep him bound, and hinder him from going to it, leaving him to die with thirst? Yet this is what is usually done at this day. Let us all agree in the way, as we agree in the end, whereof none can doubt without error. The way hath its *beginning*, its *progress*, and its *end* or mark. The more one advanceth towards the mark, the more of necessity he departeth from the beginning: and it is impossible to arrive at the mark or end, but by departing continually farther from the beginning; no one being able to go from a gate to a distant place without passing through the intermediate space. This is incontestable. If the end be good, holy, and necessary, and if the gate be good, why shall the

the way which cometh from this gate, and leadeth directly to this end, be evil? O the blindnefs of the greateft part of men, who value themfelves for their learning and wit! O how true is it, my God, that *thou haft hidden thy fecrets from the great and from the wife, to reveal them to the little ones!*

LETTERS.

LETTERS.

LETTER I.

Madam GUION to Mr. B. of LONDON.

In which is a beautiful illustration, from the similitude of a Tulip-Root.

"YOU desire that God should be the principal and only motive of your inclinations and actions, but this you will never attain to by (mere) vocal prayers, it is attainable only by a long and inde-

indefatigable perseverance in mental prayer; which you must continue by the easy means you have taken, and it will come by degrees. You see we cannot silence ourselves when we please, it is God that gives us this state of mind; * all that we can do on our part is, strenuously to *recollect ourselves*, and reunite (as *David* says) *all the powers of our soul in the Lord.* † And when the soul is thus gathered within itself and recollected, it may address itself to its God in some little affectionate breathings of the heart, just as they come in the mind, and afterwards keep in a silent respect before him; and now and then renew its affections if it finds a facility in doing it, if not, let it be altogether silent.

God

---

* Prov. xvi. 1. *The preparations of the heart man, &c. are from the Lord.*
† Psal. ciii. 1.

God has two ways of filencing the foul; the one by giving it *inwardly* *a tafte of his prefence* (but this tafte i pure, fimple, general;) the othe by making it *feel in itfelf a certain drynefs* or *inability* of producing thef acts of affection; and in that caf we ought to remain before God ii a fpirit of faith and abfolute refig nation, leaving ourfelves entirel to our Lord to deal with us as h pleafes. All depends upon th perfeverance; never therefor ceafe from prayer, although yo think you do nothing in it, for ¿ that time your humble patience i infinitely well pleafing to God nay *it is then* that God operates mc in your foul, though in a manne hidden and unknown to you fenfes. This manner of prayer not fubject to delufion or enthu fiafm for faith embraces the whol and does not expect, or defire an

thir

thing for itself. This faith has but one object, which is God, his glory and his good pleasure, which it prefers to all self-interests, and this it is that produces the pure love which loves the *whole of God*, both what he is, and for the sake of himself, without any regard to what we ourselves are.

The *silence* which some persons profess and recommend, is vastly wide of this; they are people that keep themselves still, purely in *expectation of some light, some speech*, or some new *sentiment*, and thus not seeking God for himself; they are exposed to the enemy, who deceives them by giving them a thousand extraordinary things, which are very far from the way we speak of, which is simple, humble, little; which expects nothing as believing it merits nothing; and which is persuaded that every thing extra-

extraordinary is an obstacle to the *pure* enjoyment of God. Continue therefore and persevere in your prayer be it barren or fruitful, hard or easy, all is equal to him who wills only the will of God; and who comes to God, only that God may do with him according to his pleasure. It would be a deplorable instance of inconstancy to be varying from this way under pretence that we must proceed now on this fashion, now on another. God *proves* the fidelity of the soul by these *vicissitudes*, as he does by temptations and the fear of mistaking; but provided you humbly persevere you have nothing to fear for the devil can take no hold o you: but those who desire extraordinary *gifts* and *favours* become the sport of devils.

I do not doubt but there have been and now are, among th above

above mentioned, many well-meaning people, who by their credulity have left themselves open to delusion; for the natural man always loves the marvellous, he would fain see, feel, know and discern, either his own operations, or those of some foreign agent; and this may deceive him. But he that humbly continues before God, not waiting in expectation of any thing, as well knowing he merits nothing, but is content with whatever God pleases to do, or not to do, in him or with him, is highly well pleasing to God.

I think we ought always to have some outward business that is innocent, for the mind of man is not capable of a continued introversion and abstraction; and when we begin too eagerly, it seldom lasts. We must amuse our senses *like children,* with things that are in-

nocent in themselves; and this little, humble, procedure, will draw down upon us the tender mercies of our God: who has told us that *unless we become as little children, we shall not enter into the kingdom of heaven.* Violence in this case, if it be too strong and too continual will ruin our health, and deprive us of the designs of God, who does all his works after a manner worthy of himself, though it is true he does not make our senses privy to them. Of this we may see many instances in nature. The root of a tulip, hid in the ground, seems to be but a very insignificant thing, yet when the season is come, it produces a flower of various colours, and very beautiful to the eye. If a man that had heard of a tulip but had never seen one, should be told that that bulb would produce so beautiful a flower, he would
scarce

scarce believe it; and if through his impatience he would be often taking up his tulip root out of the earth to see the process, whether it began to shoot or no, he would certainly incapacitate it for putting forth and producing this excellent flower. And, thus it is with us,* when we will be *seeing, discerning, and knowing* WHAT God operates in us, we only hinder his work. There is nothing wanting on our part but *fidelity, patience, submission, and absolute resignation* to our divine gardiner; who in his own time will let us see the wonderful things he hath wrought in us, while we thought ourselves poor, miserable, and destitute of all good.

Our failings and miseries should not

---

* Mark iv. 26. *So is the kingdom of God, as if a man should cast seed into the ground.*— Eccles. xi. 4. *He that observeth the wind shall not sow; and he that regardeth the clouds, shall not reap.*

not keep us from prayer, but o
the contrary, we should then go t
God, and say to him with an hum
ble grief, " My God! behold wha
I am capable of; if thou leave m
to myself, I shall still do worse
my whole dependence is upon th
grace; for of myself I am nothin
but misery and sin." A little chil
that is fallen in the dirt, you see
comes immediately to its mother
who makes it clean, and eve
wipes away the tears from its eyes
and thus God deals with us, whe
we fall thro' frailty; if we present
ly return to him with all our heart
David who knew the necessity o
acting thus, in this case, says t
God, *" Wash me and I shall be clean
purge me and I shall be whiter tha
snow."* It is the blood of the Lamb
without spot that can make us pure
and he will do it when we return
to him in an humble confusion fo
ou

our miseries. There is nothing in this of extraordinary performances nor high flights; what I mean is, the pure prayer of the heart.

Take courage and follow the little path, I have here shewn you, without aspiring to greater things; for be assured, it is nothing but a passion for our own excellency, that makes us so forward to change our course, or to advance of ourselves, according to our own fond conceptions, whereby instead of proceeding we go backward, and oftentimes loose all by grasping at too much.

I pray God to illuminate, and give you to understand this letter. I must however warn you (it is of the utmost consequence) to die to all spiritual *sensibilities* and curious enquiries, that so you may enter into an implicit faith, *which believeth all things*

things*—for your will must die to all tastes and sentiments, by a continual resignation, receiving and acquiescing in that inwardly, which God gives or does not give, and in that outwardly, which happens to us from moment to moment by the hand of providence; and so accustom yourself never to will that which you have not. Upon the practice of this continual submission of the will to God, depends all the progress of the spiritual life, and the good of the soul: this is *that* which will give you a perfect repose in the will of God: this is *that* which our Lord Jesus Christ hath bid us pray for, *thy will be done in earth as it is in heaven.* It is done in heaven without resistance, and without reluctance. All the outward works that we can do, be they what they will, will not, cannot,

---

* 1 Cor. xiii. 7.

cannot, advance us, as this *total* and *continual* submission of our will to the divine, most infallibly will. It is this renunciation of ourselves that Jesus Christ taught us, viz. to submit continually our *reason* to *faith* and our will to God. And this is what I require of you, that you simply enter into this course: which you see is a work of time.— Faith brings us back to our own nothingness, and by our not being any thing, leaves God to be all that he is in himself and for himself. Love is the consequence of faith: the more simple and naked the faith is, the more pure is the love: and on the other hand, faith is the consequence of love; the more perfect love is, the more perfect is faith. In the way of which I here speak and have wrote so much, we are screened from the *angel of darkness*, *who can transform himself into an angel*

gel of light: but not into an angel of love. Let us defcend by love faith, humility: keeping ourfelves in our own nothingnefs, and we need not fear falling. I require of you in the name of God, that you preferve an inviolable attachment to this way, without *wavering*. I affure you, that they who purfue this method are founded upon the living *rock, Chrift Jefus.* The devil puts doubts and uncertainties into the foul, in order to make it fickle and *inconftant*, and to keep it from perfevering, becaufe he knows great good will accrue to the foul thereby, and that this divefts him of all his right and power over it. Wherefore he ftirs up all the world to prevent, if poffible, any one's following Jefus Chrift in this path, which he himfelf traced out to us.

April, 1714.

LETTER II.

Madam GUION to Mrs. T. of LONDON.

YOUR letter, my most dear sister in our Lord, gave me such an intimacy with your heart, as very much rejoiced me. I would not have you wonder, that you have not the sweet recollection you formerly had, and that perceptible presence which God gives in the *beginnings* to those he would draw to himself. When once he has settled them in his love, and made their heart sure to him, he severs them from all this to make them walk in faith and in the cross. This first estate is *that of milk*, which St. Paul speaks of, and the second is the *bread of strong men*. In the first God gives many testimonies of his love: in the second he requires proofs of yours. He deals with us after this manner for many reasons. *First*, to the intent we may not be wedded to any consolation, but purely and nakedly to him alone, and thereby, as we ought, follow Jesus Christ, by the way of the cross. A *second* reason is, because self love nourishes itself with those things though we do not perceive it. A *third* reason is, to make us walk in naked and obscure faith, and in a love of God pure and disengaged of all self-interest, loving him above *all gifts and recompenses*, not willing any thing of God for ourselves but *his most holy will*, and not desiring any thing but purely *his glory*, even when it is to our own cost. But the *principal reason* is to

draw

draw us *out of ourselves*, and make us die to all that is of the *old man*, that so we may be cloathed, animated and vivified by the new man. Faith deprives us of all created light, whether it be of reason or laboured explanations of the pure and naked truth; without which faith, we shall never be renewed and regenerated. The pure love of God destroys in us all sorts of affections and desires, all wills, tastes and sentiments, to the end we may receive no impressions but from the will of God alone. This is the *faith* which worketh true poverty of spirit, and this is the *love* which separates us from all things, and from ourselves;— account yourself happy then inasmuch as God treats you as he did his own Son, who in the extremest outward sufferings was in the most extreme inward desolations, when he cried out, *My God, my God, why haſt thou forſaken me.* All devotion which does not tend to make us conformable to Jeſus Chriſt, I am a little ſuſpicious of; but where I ſee the croſs and deſolation, it fills my heart with joy.

I own it is a hard leſſon to be bound to hear all the trifling diſcourſes of the creatures. We ought *patiently to bear* all which belongs to our ſtate, or that come to us by providence; but where we can avoid converſation, we ſhould do all we can to ſhun it. Solitude is indeed highly agreeable to the heart that loves God, but when we are debarred of it by providence, and not of choice, we ſhould bear with patience, and for the love of him, what thoſe things ſeem to deprive us of. The true tendenc tendency which God gives to a heart loving him is *simplicity* and *littleness*. He is not truly honoured but by *children*, and *they* only *render him perfect praise*. I am very glad that you have an inclination for littleness.

When shall we be so little as not to perceive ourselves, nor be remarkable to others; when shall we be all infantine! I own to you, that all that is great in religion, does not suit me; ah! but the infancy gives me great pleasure. I never think myself well but with those that are, or are willing to become, children.

I pray, God may be all things to you, and that he himself, and *not his gifts*, may be your strength and your support; believe me in him your's: defiring with al heart, that we may be in him, for time and etern

July 24, 1714.

Two LETTERS,

CONCERNING

A Life truly Christian.

AND,

A Discourse upon the *universal* love and goodness of God to mankind, in and through Jesus Christ.

Extracted from two late Authors.

LETTER I.

Concerning a Life truly Christian.

IF we read the holy scriptures, and if the holy spirit gives us the understanding of what we read, we shall find that God desires nothing so much, as to communicate himself to men, to dwell in them as in his true temple, and to have (humanly speaking) as familiar an intercourse with them, nay, with greater intimacy and confidence, than a husband hath with his spouse, whom he loves tenderly, and with whom he shares his heart, and the goods he possesses. This the holy scriptures are full of, especially the writings of St. *John*, and the *Song of Songs*;—*Wisdom delights to be*, or to abide, *with the children of men* Prov. viii. 31. 'Tis therefore a treasure, and an honour we ough to aspire after, to become experimentally *acquainted* with the monarch of the universe, our good God, who is love itself. It is in and by an intimate commerce with our God and Saviour Jesu Christ, that we acquire those inclinations

clinations, and learn to love and practise quite naturally, and without labour, what he loved and practised: who from an excess of love for us, assumed the human nature; not to enjoy its gratifications and pleasures, its honours, riches, and grandeur in this world; but to be despised, to live in poverty, to lead a suffering and hidden life, and at last to die on the cross, filled with ignominy and the bitterest pains, and all this out of love for us: we must then, from a reciprocal love, follow a God who hath so much love for us.---It is in and by an intimate commerce with him, that we are made *partakers of the divine nature*, 2 Pet. i. 4. that we *put off the old man*, our old inclinations, and earthly and carnal affections; and that we require the grace to become citizens of heaven, even in this world. Phil. iii. 20.

20.—But a great many souls that desire to love and serve God, give themselves much trouble, labour hard and long, without advancing, for want of taking the right road to arrive thereat.—The place where we may find our Lord Jesus Christ (who is the *light* or *gift of God* to *every* man*) is our own *heart*. The *kingdom of God*, where he dwelleth, is *within* us, says, Jesus Christ. (Luke 17.) This is the place where we may infallibly meet this faithful friend and guide: it is no where else. " O! how are
" numbers of souls to be pitied,
" who from the beginning of their
" life to the end, make not one
" step in the way of the spirit;
" seeking God without, when they
" have him within themselves.
" —St. Austin complained of this,
" with respect to himself. *Lord I*
" *went*

* John i. 9.

"went wandering like a strayed sheep, seeking thee with anxious reasoning without, whilst thou wast within me; I wearied myself much in looking for thee without, and yet thou hast thy habitation within me, if I long and breath after thee. I went round the streets and places of the city of this world, seeking thee: and found thee not; because in vain I sought without for him, who was within myself." (Solilogy, chap. 31.)

The way or means to find *Christ in us*, (Col. i. 27.) is the prayer of the heart: for this is a capital truth, CHRIST IN US, AND HIS MANIFESTATION IN US, IS THE BASIS OF CHRISTIANITY. It is known only to those who are so happy as to experience it, that this truth is as real as it is unknown to those who do not experience it, who know God and religion, and all divine things, only by the way of of reasoning and speculation. Hence it comes that we see so little real fruit among Christians, who nevertheless know very well how to speak and reason about religious matters, and have a great deal of knowledge. This comes from their not having learned to *love*, without which all the rest is but a vain science. You may say perhaps, But how does one learn to love God? —It is my greatest trouble that I do not love him enough. I answer however, that prayer is the properest means: But by the word prayer, little else is understood by most people, but *vocal prayer*, or the *words* that we address to God. —I think it necessary to explain this matter a little. Our Lord tells us, that *we ought to pray always* (Luke xviii. 1.) and St. Paul says *pray without ceasing* (1 Thess. v. 17.) and also in another place, *that we know* not *what to pray for as we ought; but the spirit itself maketh intercession for us with groans that cannot be uttered,* Rom. viii. 26. Our Lord says, *Use not many words, as the Heathens do, who think they shall be heard for their much speaking.* (Mat. vi. 7.) These instructions, *to pray without ceasing, and not to use many words in our prayers,* would contradict each other, if prayer consisted only of words, either by form, or even extempore only; which could not be performed *continually* or *without ceasing.*—*Prayer* then, must be some other thing, if it can or ought to be *continual;* and that which we have just spoke of, (which is very good, provided it is used with moderation) is but one *kind* of *prayer.*

I take it then that prayer in itself is an inclination of the heart towards him, who is the object we desire to love. It is an action of
the

the heart, which is altogether natural to man; for it is natural to the heart to love, and to incline towards the object of its love. We love inceffantly; and though we lay hold on different objects on which we beftow our love, sometimes on one, and sometimes on another, and moft commonly on ourfelves, who are our principal end, and to which we would refer every other thing; yet we *always* love, and experience by our inconftancy, and by the little fatisfaction we find in the objects we choofe, that our hearts want to be filled with fomething more excellent than all the creatures together; and that it is God alone in whom this fulnefs and fatisfaction are to be found.—Therefore in order to pray aright, one needs only turn away his heart from all the creatures and himfelf, and bend it to

wards God; and this sweet exercise may be performed continually, and without *labour*. There is none necessary in order to remain quiet in the presence of a friend in whom we perfectly confide; now and then we speak to him, then we are silent; afterwards we look at him, and with gladness and satisfaction enjoy his presence, we possess him, and it is satisfaction enough to us to know that he is present. Let us thus behave towards God; though our senses do neither see nor comprehend him, we know that he is always present, filling all things; but after a particular manner, he is in the hearts of all those to whom he has already given the grace to desire to love him. This grace, if but very weak and imperfect, is from him, and is his operation, and none of ours, who *are not able of ourselves to have one good thought*. Let us be persuaded that
P God

God is more nearer to us than we are to ourselves. Let us accuſtom ourſelves to do all our actions in his preſence, and for the love of him. Let us offer up to him with an inward glance of our ſoul, all that we do, think and ſpeak. Thus ſhall we accuſtom ourſelves by degrees *to walk in his preſence.* Moreover let us uſe the means which by experience we find to be moſt efficacious for recalling the remembrance of God, and awakening his love in our hearts. And as ſoon as we perceive a forgetfulneſs of God, let us return to him inwardly and calmly, without troubling or diſquieting ourſelves. When we commit faults, let us have recourſe immediately to him; let neither fear nor ſhame hinder us from preſenting ourſelves before him, how filthy and impure ſoever we feel ourſelves to be. Let us use such reading as may draw us to him: the holy scripture is the book of books: there are others which may be a great help: we are sensible enough of those which inflame the heart and nourish it, which is always preferable to what fills the mind with images and ideas, which often consume the heart instead of feeding it. By this procedure we form a commerce in our inward man with God, which by degrees becomes continual, by frequently addressing him with the mouth or in spirit, some little word, and laying open before him with confidence our present disposition and state, as to a most faithful friend, either by a single sigh, or barely looking up to him.—If we apply ourselves to this holy exercise of walking and living in his presence, of speaking to him rather with the *heart* than the *mouth*, though *vocal prayer* is very commendable too at certain times, *when we find it suits our present state:* if we do this, we shall soon find a great change in ourselves; that the love of God shall take possession of our hearts, and disengage us more and more from ourselves and the creatures. The whole business consists in turning away, the most we can, our thoughts, from every thing that is not God; employing ourselves quietly and calmly with God present, without pretending to form distinct ideas of him. Thus shall we be made capable, and disposed to receive a thousand graces and favours from him. This attention does not consist in expecting to hear some extraordinary voice with our bodily ears.—God does not speak after that manner, his language is to the heart.—The change of inclinations desires and affections,

tions, which we experience by degrees, from earthly and carnal, to become more and more heavenly and divine, is the language of Christ in us: he creates and operates what he speaks, all at the same time; we do not hear his voice with our ears, but we experience the effects of it.—He loves *silence, retirement,* and *recollection.* In this disposition he makes himself manifest to, and felt by the heart, in a manner incomprehensible to human reason. *There* he teaches us inwardly, in so real and efficacious a manner, that when we experience it, we perceive that all the voices that strike our senses outwardly, however good, have not the efficacy, the reality of what we experience within us. Therefore it is that our Lord saith, Matt. 23. *One is your teacher.* It is because his voice alone is able to operate in us what he teaches us.

It may be objected, if so it be that the voice of God, or what they would have us to believe to be such, is not a voice which one hears with his bodily ears, why do they so earnestly recommend *silence, retirement, recollection*, and to avoid the distractions of the mind? What matters it what the senses be employed about? I answer, that though the voice of God to the soul, doth not with its sound strike the senses, yet it requires recollection, and avoiding distractions, if it is to operate with efficacy in our hearts; because the distractions and dissipation of the senses among various objects, are the very things which draw away the *will* and the *love*, and beget an attachment to those objects which the senses present to us; they are the windows of the soul, and the gates by which the creatures enter into it. Therefore,

fore, as *soon* as the soul has a
desire of being converted to God,
and of loving him with all its powers; it feels within itself an inclination and bias to *retirement,* in order
to turn itself freely, and without
interruption towards its God; and
to follow the good motions he
vouchsafes, and what the conscience dictates to be the things that
draw it to him, and disengage it
from the creatures: these are the
effects of what he operates or speaks
in the bottom of the heart: his language is conformable to his spiritual
nature, and makes itself to be understood by our spirit, which is also
of the same nature;—*God is spirit,
and the true worshippers worship him
in spirit,* John 3. The more we
advance in the ways of God, and
follow the good motions of his spirit in our hearts, the more is this
matter unfolded, and the *hidden man*
of

of the heart, (1 Pet. iii. 4.) made manifest, which is as it were buried in the senses, as long as they have dominion over us. Therefore it hath been the practice of all the saints in all ages to mortify their senses.—And every saint in every age hath testified, that it is *our own experience alone* that can explain to us what that life of the spirit is, of which St. Paul speaks when he says, (Rom. 8.) *They that are after the flesh, do mind the things of the flesh, and they that are after the spirit the things of the spirit.*

MAY 14, 1735.

LETTER II.

Describing some of the temptations which attend a life truly Christian.

" THAT which hinders the progress of the divine life in most well disposed persons, is, their resting too much not only in externals, but more especially in that which is *internal*, namely, the sentiments, consolations, and fervours, which God communicates for encouraging young beginners to walk in the way of *self denial*, and to pass on further. God gives them these sensibilities, not that they may rest in them, but in order to their further progress: he gives them because of our want of faith and confidence in him, above all these

these sweetnesses; to which we must absolutely die, if we would attain the *true good*. Souls in that state knowing nothing better, and more profound, God withdraws those sensibilities after a certain space of time; in which the soul ought to have acquired strength and courage enough to abandon herself to the conduct of God; which is what he proposes by withdrawing all those consolations and fervours that allure and render her sensual and dainty. But when the soul is deprived thereof, she supposes all is lost. Many drawback at this time, and return to the love of this present evil world: others stop short for want of courage, who continue languishing all their life long, without *entering into the true rest promised to the children of God* (Heb. iv. 5) always in anguish, vexation, and uncertainty. Others entirely

entirely neglect *internal* prayer, and content themselves to live like other folks, and look upon all that formerly past within them like unto pleasant *dreams*; and consider others, who still enjoy these sweet consolations and lively sentiments, as harmless, innocent people, but of weak understanding, whom they pity. All this proceeds from their not having at the beginning laid a good foundation, and set out in the only *path* that leads to God: I mean, living by *faith* and resignation to God; entirely surrendering themselves into his hands without prescribing any terms. This is that good foundation, which cannot be shaken; namely, the unreserved surrendering ourselves into the hands of God; willing nothing but *him*, and the accomplishment of his will; renouncing all consolations and self-gratifications,

ons, both outward and inward accepting as it were by the by without resting in them, all those that the divine bounty shall think fit to give; valuing nothing but him, and willing nothing but his *will*. This is the self-denied life which will infallibly conduct us to the true good, or the *manifestation of Jesus Christ in us*.—When it pleases God to drain this source of consolations, that nourished the soul for a time, and filled her with courage to combat and despise the world and all earthly things; when I say, all this forsakes us, and nothing succeeds but languishment weakness and aversion to continue in that course of life, which we had embraced with so much eagerness and relish; finding nothing now in ourselves to supply the place of those sensibilities which are withdrawn from us, the soul knows no where

where she is; and as I said, all that is past seems to her like a pleasant dream: the enemy at the same time conspiring with her reason, discovers to her many excesses into which she has given, intoxicated as she was with the heat of her zeal, and makes her to call in question the whole of Christian experience.—She knows not what to do: all is disgusting and wearisome to her. O! how dangerous is this rock, against which many have struck, and been fatally shipwrecked! Many fall here into libertinism, if their constitution inclines thereunto: for having already seen the insufficiency of all outward forms of worship, they now find nothing therein to support themselves; and the enemy making them likewise to suspect the internal ways, the truth and reality of which is obscured and hid from

them at this time, they fall into licentioufnefs, and become, or are in danger of becoming Atheifts; or elfe are in danger of falling a prey to feducing fpirits, that fail not to offer themfelves both inwardly and outwardly, promifing liberty, tho' themfelves are the flaves of Satan, or of their own fpirit. *Reafon* is the moft dangerous enemy at this time, to thofe, who before their converfion led a wife and virtuous life according to the world: and it eafily draws the foul into its ancient way of living, making her to fhut the gate againft all the internal *attractions* of the fpirit o grace, which difturb and difquie her, and are defigned to make her fenfible by the trouble they excite that fhe is in no good ftate.— *Thefe* are fome of the dreadfu dangers and temptations that affaul the foul in this ftate: they canno
al

all be defcribed, becaufe of their diverfity and number.—How many doubts, difquiets, fears and terrors, do affault the poor foul! On the other hand, with what levity and rafhnefs is fhe tempted to plunge headlong into the world, into libertinifm ; and to give wing to her paffions that had been reftrained for a time. Who is able to efcape fo great a danger! God alone can defend and fecretly fupport us, who never fails to do it, provided the foul doth but even feebly look unto him ; for he hath promifed to *ftrengthen the feeble knees, and that the bruifed reed he will not break.* —He mercifully reclaims her, though fhe have gone aftray for fome time, from which few, very few, are altogether exempt, and many remain bewildered, wandering hither and thither, without finding the peace and repofe they feek after for many years: but God brings them again into the right way, by fome violent temptation, or extraordinary accident, which incites them a new to have recourfe to God, who alone can help and deliver, and give them folid peace.—Thofe are infallibly fafe, who, under this ftate of uncertainty, fo painful and troublefome to bear, remain in peace and tranquility, without *undertaking* or *altering* any thing in their conduct or ftate: for they are not in a condition to fee clearly: all is darknefs or obfcurity—therefore cannot but miftake and fail in any thing they undertake during that period. They are bleffed indeed! to whom God at this time fends fome *experienced* perfon, who hath himfelf paffed thefe dangerous ftreights, and has been faved from being fhipshipwrecked therein, who is capable of giving proper counsel, provided they are humble, and willing to accept it. The best advice for this state is this. *" Be patient, remain in peace, stillness and tranquility, amidst all your trouble, anxiety, and inconstancy: pursue not any of those things to which your disposition to inquietude, impatience, and the like, would hurry you: wait patiently for the assistance of our blessed Lord, and support the delay of it, without seeking after, or accepting any pretended help that may offer from any other quarter."* This is a painful lesson for nature, which is so much the more so, because the soul doth not perceive it is to God that she resigns herself, but is afraid, and believes rather that it is owing to its own negligence, stupidity and sloth, that all this is fallen upon her. But whosoever will be courageous enough to surrender himself up to God, in silence and refignation, fuffering and bearing all the inward burnings and remorfes that torment him: *perfevering* to wait patiently, expecting help from no other but God, fhould fuch a one *die in this* ftate, he would find the favour and unexpected help of our adorable Jefus, to whom be honour and glory throughout all eternity. Amen.

A

DISCOURSE

UPON THE

Univerfal Love and goodnefs of God to Mankind in and through Jefus Chrift.

IT is the fundamental doctrine, or rather the *known* foundation of all *revealed* religion, and the *unknown* foundation of all natural piety and goodnefs, that Jefus Chrift is the *Second Adam.*

That a real birth, life, and nature, is in the fame *reality* derived to us us from this our second Adam, as is derived to us from our first Adam. And that as without any figure or metaphor, we are all said to be born of *Adam*, and descended from him; so we are all really and not figuratively born of our second Adam, and have our descent from him. And herein is seen the infinite depth of divine love and goodness to mankind, who though they were by the condition of their creation to be derived from one *head* or *parent*, and take his state of perfection or imperfection; yet were by the goodness and care of God for them, provided from the very beginning, with a second *parent*, or common *head*, who after the *fall* of the first, and the fallen state that he had brought upon his posterity, should be a *common restorer*, and put it in every man's power to have the same choice

choice of life and death, as the firft man had; that fo, they who were loft before they were born, and were made inheritors of a miferable nature without their choice, might have a divine life reftored to them in a *fecond* parent, which fhould not be in the power of any one to lofe for them, but fhould depend entirely upon their *own will* and *defire of it,* upon their *own faith,* and *hope,* and *hungering* after it.

This eternal and immutable truth, worthy of being written in capital letters of gold; is fuch as is fufficient to make all men rejoice and give praife to God. For by this truth, all that feems hard and cruel to human reafon, that the pofterity of *Adam* fhould be involved in the confequences of their firft father's fall, is made a wonderful fcene of love.—There is something so amazingly loving and merciful in this conduct of divine providence over mankind, that it has surely enough in it, if once known, to make revealed religion the joy, and comfort, and desire of every man's heart. That Jesus Christ is thus the Saviour and universal Redeemer of all mankind, that he is this *Second Adam*, or parent, restoring *Adam* himself, and in him all mankind to a possibility of being born again; and that revealed religion *began* with the *declaration* of this redemption, and has revealed nothing but for the sake and support of it, is a truth sufficiently attested by scripture.

The declaration which God made to *Adam* immediately after his *fall*, of a *seed of the woman to bruise the serpent's head*, was a declaration of *pardon* and *redemption* to *Adam*, and in him to all mankind; for

for what he said to *Adam*, that he said to all that were in the loins of *Adam*; who, as they fell in his fall, before they were born, without the possibility of any one man's being exempted from it; so were they all put into this state of pardon and redemption before they were born, without the possibility of any one man's being excluded, or left out of it.

Every son of *Adam* is in the same covenant with God that *Adam* was, and has the same *bruiser* of the serpent as *near* to him, as he was to *Adam*, and declared to be his Redeemer, in the same degree as he was declared to be the Redeemer of *Adam*. And who would seek for arguments against such a Saviour? Or who would cavil at a *revealed religion*, that has no other beginning or end, but to reveal an *universal redemption*? Or who can enough call upon

upon the creation, heaven and earth, angels and men, and every thing that hath breath, to praise the Lord, for such salvation? This declaration of God to *Adam*, of his pardon, and redemption by the seed of the woman, is not to be considered, as we consider the *declaration* of a *pardon* made by some great *prince* to an offending *subject*, which is only a declaration of *words*, that are heard only with our outward ears, and of a person that is entirely distinct from us.

God's pardoning a sinner, or redeeming fallen man, has nothing like this in it. This declaration to *Adam*, and in him to all mankind, is not the declaration of a being that is *out of*, or separate from us, but of a God in whom *we live and move, and have our being*; who is, the life of our life, the spirit of our spirit: his declaration therefore must

must signify some inward *change,* or new *state* of our existence in him, or that *he is* to us, and in us, that which *he was not* before he pardoned us.

When therefore God said to *Adam* and *Eve, The seed of the woman shall bruise the head of the Serpent,* it had the same effect, as if he had said, *Be ye henceforth in a state of salvation, and let the redeeming conquering seed of the woman, from this time, begin to have power in you, and be in you, a strength against the Serpent.* This declaration was not *solely* a promise of something to come, but of something then *inwardly* done and *given,* by a God inwardly present in him, and signified no less than God's *seeking* and *manifesting* himself again to a creature, that had *lost* him as his God and *only good.* - And was the real *communication* of something to

Adam, which made him *capable* of enjoying God as his *good*. Had not God at that time, done *inwardly* in the *depth* of his foul, something like that which he did to the darkness of the deep, when he spoke light into it, *Adam* and *Eve*, and *all* their posterity, had been inwardly meer *devils*, and outwardly mere *beasts*.—For had not God thus in the beginning of the fall, before any man was born into the world of *Adam* and *Eve*, spoke pardon and redemption unto *Adam* and *Eve*; neither they, nor any of their posterity had been *capable* of any *desire* of God, but had lived as much without all *conscience*, or *instinct* of goodness, as the beasts of the earth and devils do.

Therefore God at that time, *communicated* to man, a *desire*, a *capacity* to enjoy him as his *only good*, by sowing into him a *seed* of the woman

man, a *spark* of life, an *inſtinct* of goodneſs, a *taſte* of heaven, a *principle* of holineſs, a *touch* of love, the *pearl* of the goſpel, the *pledge*, of immortality, the *hidden kingdom* of God.—All which expreſſions, are inſufficient to expreſs that *inward treaſure* of the ſoul, which God in the beginning of the redemption, or as his act of redemption, communicated to man.

And in this degree of redemption is every creature that is born of Adam; he has this kingdom of God in his ſoul, as a *grain* of *muſtard ſeed*, a *ſpark* of life, a *pledge*, of immortality, and *attraction* to God! If he *tramples* this *pearl* under his feet; then his deſtruction is from himſelf; but if he will co-operate with that *inward Redeemer* which God has put into his ſoul, if he will ſuffer his ſpark to *kindle*, his *inſtinct* of goodneſs to *ſpread* itſelf, the light of life to *arife* in him, the voice of God to be *heard* in him; then will the *divine* life, be brought forth in him; and when his body dies, he will fall into all the fulnefs of God.

And now, my dear reader, how fhall I touch your heart? Or how can your heart be untouched with this affecting view of the mercies of God in Chrift Jefus, and of the riches and treafures which lie hid in your own foul, wanting nothing but your own confent and good wifhes to be manifefted in you?

If you rejeƈt the *Saviour* offer'd to you in the gofpel, you rejeƈt *all that* which makes you differ from a *devil*; for that offered Saviour, is that very fame *inward light of your mind*, which makes you now differ from a devil.

To refufe him therefore that fpeaketh to you in the gofpel, is
rejeƈting

rejecting *all* that God has ever *transacted* with man; it is renouncing all that is *divine* and *good* within you; it is saying that you will have no benefit from the *good workings* or motions in your own heart; for Jesus Christ that calls you to repentance in the gospel, is the *very same* blessed Saviour, that *warns, reproves* and *preaches* repentance in the inmost essence of your spirit.

But, my friend, be wise in time, for this goodness will continue but for a time; and if you die rejecting the benefits of Christ, you will be without Christ, and you will find that all is gone with him, and that you will have nothing left, but that nature which is the torment of hell. If therefore you reject Christ in the utmost efforts of his goodness to save you, you will find that the renouncing of Christ, is renouncing all that you have

have from him, and that nothing is left in that soul, where he is not, but mere darkness.

But, to return to my subject; what I have said above of God's covenant with *Adam*, is God's covenant with all mankind, and therefore thus far all mankind are the redeemed of Jesus. There is no partiality in God. As all *fell* and *died* in *Adam*, so all were *restored* in his restoration. Thus says the apostle, *As by the offence of one, judgment came upon all to condemnation;* EVEN SO BY *the righteousness of one, the free gift came upon all men* UNTO JUSTIFICATION OF LIFE. Rom. v. 18. And the gospel expresly saith, that Jesus Christ is the *true light which lighteth every man that cometh into the world.* Therefore Jesus Christ is in every man that cometh into the world, and every son of *Adam* has received ed *that same* from Jesus Christ, which Adam received from him, viz. An *inward light of life,* a *beginning* of his salvation, an actual *power* to resist the serpent; and Jesus Christ is, and ever was, the *free gift of God unto all men.*

HEATHENS, JEWS, and CHRISTIANS, differ only in this, that one and the same Saviour is *differently* made known to them.—The Heathens knew him not as he was manifested to the Jews, nor as he is gloriously manifested in the gospel; but they knew him as he was the God of their *hearts,* manifesting himself by a *light* of the mind, by a *sensibility* of guilt, by *awakenings* and *warnings* of conscience; and this was their gospel, which they received as really in and by *Jesus Christ,* as the law and gospel were received thro' him. Therefore it is a great and glorious truth, enough
to

to. turn every voice into a trumpet, and make heaven and earth ring with praises and hallelujahs to God, that Jesus Christ is the Saviour of all the world, and of every man of every nation, kindred, and language. Therefore saith St. *John, They sung a new song, saying, Thou art worthy to take the book, and to open the seals thereof; for thou wast slain, and hast redeemed us to God by thy blood, out of every kindred, and tongue, and people, and nation.* Rev. v. 9. And again, *After this, I beheld,* says he, *and lo, a great multitude, which no man could number, of all nations and kindreds, and people, and tongues, stood before the throne, and before the Lamb, cloathed with white robes, and with palms in their hands, and cried with a loud voice, saying, Salvation to our God which sitteth upon the throne, and unto the Lamb.* Rev. vii. 9, 10.

Every Heathen, Jew, and Christian, is forced to know and feel, whether he will or no, that God has a certain *secret power* within him, which is watching every opportunity of saying something to him, either of himself, the vanity of the world, or the guilt and consequences of sin. This is that instinct of goodness, attraction of God, or witness of himself in every man, which without arguments and reasonings rises up in the soul, and would be doing some good to it, if not quenched and resisted by the noise and hurry either of pleasures or business.

Therefore, my dear friend, know the place of your religion, turn inwards, listen to the voice of grace, the instinct of God that speaks and moves within you; let your heart pray to God, to bring forth his own divine nature in you. Your heart wants

wants nothing but God, and nothing but your heart can receive him. This is the only place and feat of religion, and of all communication between God and you.

This *free gift* of God to all men, has that natural fitnefs for the receiving of Chrift, as the eye has for receiving the light; it wants him, it defires him, it is for him, it rejoices in him, as the eye wants, defires, and rejoices in the light. And of this, does our Saviour plainly fpeak, when he fays, *He that is of God heareth God's word*, and again, *My fheep hear my voice*.

The whole of natural religion confifts in a man's following this voice of nature, and acting conformable to it; in acknowledging the *finfulnefs* of his ftate, and in *imploring* and *relying* upon the *divine mercy* to be delivered from it; tho' it is not known by what name to call

call that deliverance, or what kind of Saviour is wanted to effect it. But he that thus according to the direction of his natural state lives before God, in *penitence,* and in *faith* in his mercy, is sure of having the benefit of all the mercy of God, though he does not know the *method,* or the *means,* by which the mercy of God will save him.—Had a man no sense of shame for his sins, he would be in the very state of the beasts; had he no *faith* and *hope* in the *mercy* of God, he would be in the state of the devils.

Therefore that internal *sentiment* of *heart,* that *instinct* of goodness, is the *preservation* of his nature, and the *saving* him from being like to the beasts and fallen spirits. And all revealed religion, is to improve this true religion of nature in its two *essential parts,* penitence for sin, and

and faith and truft in the mercy of God. For all revealed religion, intends nothing, but to give us more reafons for *penitence, faith* and *truft* in the mercy of God.

And this inftinct of good, or true religion of nature, is the *very preparation* of the heart for the reception of the gofpel. For fo much as there is of this *penitence* and *faith* living in the foul, fo much it has of eyes to fee, of ears to hear, and of a heart to underftand all the truths of divine revelation. The humility and penitence of the gofpel, the mercies of God in and through Jefus Chrift, are as agreeable to a man in this ftate of heart, as food and water to the hungry and thirfty foul. And when he finds the gofpel, he finds the pearl, for which he gladly fells all that he hath. Therefore there is the fame agreement, and the fame difference
between

between the *true* religion of nature, and the religion of the gofpel, that there is between the breaking of the day, and the rifing of the fun to its *meridian* height;—and as the light of the day-break, and the light of the noon-day, are both the fame light, and from the fame producer of light; fo the light of the religion of nature, and the light of the gofpel, are the fame light, and from the fame producer of light in the mind.

Don't therefore, my dear friend, deceive yourfelf, nor let any one elfe deceive you. The matter is of infinite confequence that you have before you. You come into the world but once, and have but one trial, but the effects of it are to laft for ever. The time of difputing and fpeculating is fhort; it can laft no longer than whilft the *fun* of this world can refrefh your flefh and blood, and so keep the soul from knowing its own depth, or what has been growing in it. But when this is over, then you must know and feel what it is to have a nature as *deep*, and *strong*, and *large* as eternity.

If you have lived upon the amusements of *reason* and speculation, your life has been worse than a *dream*, and your soul will at the end of such a life, be left to itself in its own *darkness, hunger, thirst*, and *anxiety*, to be for ever devoured by its own fire.

But if you have watched over that *instinct* of *goodness* which God planted in your soul, and have exercised yourself in that *penitence* for your sins, and humble *faith* in the *mercy* of God, that the gospel proposes to you; then when your body falls off from you, you will feel and know what a kingdom of
God

God lay hid in your foul, you will see that you have a *life* and *strength* like that of eternity, and the fulnefs of God himfelf will be your everlafting enjoyment.

You are now your own *carver*, and muft be *that* which you fhall have made of yourfelf. If the depth of your heart has not in this life's time its proper cure, if it has not fomething done to it, which your *reafon* can no more do, than it can create the light, your heart will become your hell. And if you let the light of the gofpel fhine into it, and revive the *good feed* of life in it, then it will become the feat and habitation of your heaven.

But it may be, you will fay, you would believe the gofpel if you could, but that its evidence cannot have that effect upon your mind.—As the gofpel is much defended and oppofed by learned men,

men, its evidence is so perplexed, that your mind cannot come at any certainty of what you ought to believe concerning the truth of it.

I will therefore propose the shortest, and the surest of all methods.—Now I desire you to know no books, nor to be well read in any controversy but in that which passes within you, in order to know the gospel to be the greatest of all truths, and the infallible voice of God speaking the way of salvation to you.

The gospel is built on these *two pillars, first,* That you are a *fallen:* *secondly,* That you are a *redeemed* creature. Now every man's own soul, speaks these two great truths to him. You *feel,* and *know* that you are a sinner, that you have the disorders of the beasts, and the depravity of evil spirits within you.

Is

Is not this faying to you, by the *frame* and *voice* of your nature, that you are a *fallen* creature, and not in that ftate in which a good being muft have created you? For I appeal to yourfelf, in your own degree of goodnefs, if you could create your own children, whether you would not create them in a better ftate, and with lefs evil, both of the beaft and the devil in them; than that in which you was born yourfelf.

Therefore, only fuppofing God to have your degree of goodnefs, he could not have created the firft man, from whom your nature is derived in the ftate that you are; and therefore fuppofing him only to be good, you have a fufficient proof; but fuppofing him to be infinitely good, or goodnefs itfelf, you have an infallible demonftration written in the frame of your nature, that you are a *fallen* creature, or not in that state in which God created you.

Again, do you want any learning or books, to shew you, that every man, as well as yourself, affects to appear virtuous, to have good qualities, and is ashamed of every beastly and diabolical disorder; and would seem to have virtues and goodness, that he has not, because of an innate love that he has for them; and from a sense of their being proper for him? And is not this saying again with the same fulness of certainty, that you are a *redeemed* creature, that there is in you an *inward* Redeemer, a *light* of the mind, a *seed* of goodness, an *instinct* to virtue, given you by God, though without revelation you don't know *when* nor *how* ? And do you not hereby plainly see, that you stand nearer to *the Love of God.*

to the truth of the Christian religion, than you do to any thing else? It is the book of yourself, it talks of nothing *out* of you, it speaks but that which is said *within* you, and therefore you have a sufficient help to understand it. What can the gospel say to you of the fall of man, and of your redemption, that is not at the same time said to you, by the state of your own soul?

A sinful creature, cannot come from God in its sinful state. And on the other hand, if you was not redeemed, how could you feel an inclination to goodness, and a desire of appearing virtuous? For what else is this desire, but a certain *inward* principle that has begun your *redemption*, and is trying to carry it on? Now the Christian religion tells you only this great truth, that you are *fallen* and *redeemed*,

deemed, that is, that you have a mixture of *evil*, and *good* in you. That from the beginning of the world, it has been God's gracious defire and defign in and by Jefus Chrift, to render your redemption effectual, that is, to make the *good* that is in you perfectly overcome all your *evil*. Complain therefore no more of want of evidence; you are the gofpel's *evidence*, it is preached in your own bofom. And this great and glorious truth, that I have declared: this *free gift* of God to all men, by a feed of life, which all men receive from Chrift, is the true and folid meaning of that which is called *preventing grace*, and which, when rightly fpoken of, is faid to be common to all men. It is *grace*, becaufe it is God's *free gift*, we could not lay hold of it by any power of our own, nor had any right to claim it. It
is

is *preventing grace*, becaufe it prevents or goes before, and is not given us for any thing that we have done. And therefore it has its plain diftinction from God's affifting grace.—St. Paul fays, *God hath chofen us in Chrift Jefus, before the foundation of the world.* Now from this eternal, forefeeing goodnefs of God towards mankind, it is, that a *fpark* of the firft divine life, called *a feed of the woman*, the *ingrafted* WORD, *a kingdom of God, a pearl of great price, a treafure hid in a field*, was fore-ordained to be treafured up;—which through the divine love, (my dear reader) is fecurely treafured up, as a pearl hidden in thy own field; which, if it be not thy own fault, fhall furely revive into its firft glory, through Chrift, who is, and ever fhall be, the RESURRECTION, and the

the LIFE.—This divine *feed*, or *free gift* of God. is the *general*, and *preventing grace* of all *men*, that enables them fo to act, as to obtain God's *affifting grace*, in the renewal of their hearts and minds; and it is a glorious and undeniable truth, that there is no *partiality* in God, but that *all* men, have a *general call*, and a *general capacity* to obtain their falvation.—God has but *one defign* towards all mankind: CHRISTIANS, JEWS, and HEATHENS, are all *equally* the defire of his heart,— his *wifdom crieth, fhe putteth forth her voice*, not here or there, but every where, in all the ftreets of all the parts of the world.——O my God, juft and good, how great is thy love and mercy to mankind, that heaven is thus every where open, and CHRIST thus the *common* Saviour of *all!* O fweet

power

power of the *bruiser* of the serpent, born in every son of man, that stirs and works in every man, and gives every man a power, to find his happiness in God! O holy JESUS, heavenly *light, that lightest every man that cometh into the world*, that redeemest every soul that follows thy light, which is *always within him!* O holy Trinity, immense ocean of divine love in which all mankind live, and move, and have their being! None are separated from thee, none live out of thy love, but all are embraced in the arms of thy mercy, all are partakers of thy divine life, the operation of thy holy spirit, as soon as their heart is turned to thee! O plain, and easy, and simple way of salvation, wanting no subtilties of art or science, no borrowed learning,

learning, no refinements of reason, but all done by the simple natural motion of every heart, that truly longs after God!

FINIS.

www.ingramcontent.com/pod-product-compliance
Lightning Source LLC
Chambersburg PA
CBHW031820230426
43669CB00009B/1202